From Mayhem to Maturity (almost!)

A Survival Guide for Parents of Middle School Girls

"Our youth now love luxury. They have bad manners, contempt for authority; they show disrespect for their elders and love chatter in place of exercise; they no longer rise

when elders enter the room; they contradict their parents, chatter before company; gobble up their food and tyrannize their teachers."
-- Socrates

Introduction

Socrates made this comment thousands of years ago and yet it is still true today. Middle school students are forming their own identity separate from their parents, requiring them to begin to move away from their parents and towards their peers.

The opinions of your daughter's peers will have an enormous effect on her way of thinking, dressing, and acting, which can change on a daily basis.

She will enter puberty, if she hasn't already, and will have to deal with menstruation, her first bra, and all the misinformation about sex and drugs that her classmates will teach her.

She's going to have more difficult classes and more challenging homework. She'll need your help in budgeting her time and still getting enough sleep to prepare for the next school day.

One day she'll be playing with her dolls and stuffed animals, and the next day she'll be stuck to her cell phone talking to her best friend about a boy she likes.

My Story

I volunteered at a community function recently and there was a group of students from a community college. As I talked with the young girl assigned to help me, I asked her about middle school. She was pretty and well spoken and would have good comments to add to my book, I thought. I asked her what the best and worst parts of middle school were. Her answer should not have surprised me. "I do my best to try not to remember those years."

I wasn't sure if I wanted to ask why, but I was intrigued. "Because of all the cliques. One day a group of girls liked you and made you part of their group, and the next day you were ignored and made fun of by the same girls. I hated it." I asked her if it mattered that she was a black young lady. "It made no difference what color you were. The girls were mean."

Why This Book

After I wrote and published my kindergarten books "Don't Forget Your Sunglasses: A Parent's Survival Guide to Kindergarten" and my "Start At Home" series located at http://www.amazon.com/author/kathleenbenyo, parents asked me to write a handbook for parents of middle schoolers. As I began my research, I understood why they asked for something to hold in their hands and find information and suggestions. So much is happening with and about tweens and middle school!

My intent in this handbook is to provide parents with insight into middle school girls, their personalities, their lives, their hopes and dreams and even their nightmares. This handbook also provides information for parents about areas in which they are unsure how to proceed or approach, or topics new to them. This book is for you, middle school parents of tween girls!

> *"Youth is wasted on the young."*
> --Socrates

Section Summaries

Introduction

Here you'll find out why I found it important to write this book and what my own experience has been, which also appears in other sections of this book. I have listed many websites for your convenience, but you may have to copy some and paste them into your browser. In other situations, the website may already no longer exist. For that I apologize, but the Internet is in a constant state of flux.

Testing 1-2-3 and More

In this section you'll find a quiz for you and your daughter to take before you read the book, which may lead to some interesting conversation and discovering different points of view; definition of a tween, which changes depending upon the writer and the context; how and when middle schools actually started and why, and how a good middle school should run based on my studies and experience; and the dedication, copyright, disclaimer, and about the author.

Near the end of the book you'll find the answers to the true/false quiz you and your daughter took, a list of some of my favorite fiction and nonfiction books for tweens, and a little story about a new tween.

Behaviors

They may happen quickly or so slowly it takes you a while to realize what is happening, but middle school is a time of great change for adolescents. Some behaviors will surface, ones that you have seen over the years, but now they're more pronounced, more serious, and more carefully constructed by your daughter. You will have to deal with the middle school issues of inappropriate language, talking back, lying, cheating, stealing, and trying oh so hard to influence and manipulate you. There are suggestions for handling each of these negative behaviors while gaining the trust of your daughter. You'll have to decide what matters and what you can overlook, and it won't be the same as when she was in elementary school. You'll have to be strong but caring, understanding but firm, and keep your word so your daughter knows what to expect.

Bullying

Do you know what bullying looks and sounds like? Can you tell if your daughter is being bullied? Or if she is doing the bullying? Do you know the long term effects of being bullied or doing the bullying? How can you help your daughter if she observes bullying? Do you know the signs of trouble so you can be there for your daughter?

Cell Phones

This topic gets its own section because they are so prevalent in our society. Should you allow your child to take her phone to school? Should she be allowed to have it in her bedroom? How about after lights out? Is there a limit on how long she can talk? How about what topics she can discuss? When is your involvement concern and when is it interference? Only you can answer these questions, but this section may help you.

Choose, Decide, Pick

Chuck Moorman has written about these three words and what an important part they play in the development of your child. You might have to practice using them, too.

Clothing

What should your daughter be permitted to wear to school? What's off limits? Do you know the dress policy of the school (if there is one)? How much should you spend on new clothing and where should you purchase it? What's a good way to find out what other girls are wearing before your daughter starts middle school?

Courses

This section offers a quick overview of what to expect in middle school, focusing on learning to be an independent thinker and problem solver, while your daughter realizes she's part of a very large and distinct world.

Curfew

There's a lot to consider when it comes to this section. What is the appropriate bedtime for a sixth, seventh, or eighth grader? How much sleep should your daughter get? What about weeknights? Weekends? Does your daughter understand the rules of curfew?

Clean Your Room

Don't be surprised if the floor of your daughter's bedroom is not visible underneath all of the clothes and shoes strewn there. You may instruct your daughter to clean her room. What if she doesn't do it? What could the reason be? How can you solve the problem?

Dating

This section is very short because it is discussed in detail in my second book about middle school girls, to be released shortly after this one. Think about dating and what you will and won't allow. Then find out from your daughter what she thinks dating is. You might be surprised with her answer compared to what you think. I encourage you to read my next book for detailed discussion on sex and dating, drugs and alcohol. And more.

Doctor and Dentist Visits

When should they be scheduled? What does your daughter need? What should you ask the doctor/dentist?

Dangers

Drugs, alcohol, and cigarette smoking all move to the forefront of concerns when your daughter reaches middle school, if it hasn't already. Do you know the most commonly abused drug? Do you know how kids get it? Is alcohol as popular as it seems? How can you help your daughter stay away from alcohol?

What do you do if you find cigarettes in your daughter's bag? How do you respond/react? What can these behaviors imply for later years?

Due Diligence

What is due diligence? Should I do it? How do I do it? How do I find time?

Emergency Contact

Who should you select as the emergency contact for your child? How do you decide? What does this person need to know? What does the school need to know? How can you ensure that your daughter gets medical attention she needs if you can't get to her quickly?

Home Alone

When is your daughter old enough to be left home alone? How long should she be alone? Should she be charged with caring for her younger siblings? How do you know when she's ready? What does she need to know? What do you need to do to prepare her?

Internet

Where should the computer/laptop be placed in the house? How much leisure time should your daughter spend on the Internet? How is the Internet dangerous? What can your daughter do while on the Internet to be safe? How can you ensure she is safe? What about computers in schools, libraries, and at friends' homes? What about being on the Internet with her phone? What about social media? Are you aware of the many kinds that exist? Should your daughter be a member of any of them? How do you ensure she is safe? And what are all those letters she uses when she writes a text?

Lunches

Should your daughter pack or buy? Where do you find the money to pay for school lunches? How do you ensure that her packed lunch is healthy? What types of foods should your daughter eat? And how much? How many calories each day are recommended? What if your daughter is losing weight? What if your daughter is gaining weight? Does it matter? Should you pack your daughter's lunch? When?

Make Up

Should you allow your tween to wear makeup? Should you select it or should she? What does she need to know about keeping her face clean if she's wearing makeup during the day? If she attends sports practice after school? What can be done about acne? Are there specific products that are especially helpful? What should she keep away from? Is it okay for her to share makeup with her best friend?

Questions

What are the right questions to ask your daughter? Are there wrong questions?

Parents' Roles?

Is your role the same as when your daughter was in elementary school? How do you adjust to her middle school attitudes and opinions? What should you do?

Parent/Teacher Conferences

By middle school, many students don't want their parents to go to parent conferences. They look at them as elementary activities for "babies". Should you go any way? If you go, what should you ask? What should you listen for? What should you do after the meeting?

Prepare Your Child for Middle School

How can you help your child prepare for this major change in her life? How do you let her know that you understand and are there for her? What specific activities can you do to with or for your child to make this transition less stressful?

Questions

You have experienced the frustration of asking your daughter how her day was and getting an "Okay' or a shoulder shrug in response. That's because you're asking the wrong questions. Make your questions specific so that they require responses. Here are some examples I found on Facebook (anonymous) and some of my own. You'll think of some good questions as you learn what's going on each day. There's always a drama somewhere.

- What was the best thing that happened at school today? (you might get the answer "It ended".)
- What was the worst thing that happened at school today? (you might get the answer "It started".)
- What made you laugh today?
- Who do you like to sit next to in class? Why?
- Who would you prefer not to sit by? Why?

- If I spoke with your teacher, what would he tell me about you?
- Did you help someone today? How?
- Did someone help you today? How?
- What's one thing new you learned today in class?
- What bored you today? Why?
- Who is the funniest person in your class? Does your teacher think he's funny?
- What was the best part of lunch? Why?
- If you were the teacher in (pick subject) tomorrow, what would you teach and how would you do it?
- Tell me one time you used your highlighter today.

- What's one reason you couldn't wait to come home?
- Do you have a lot of homework? What are you going to tackle first? Why?
- How was your (subject) test? What was on it that you didn't expect?
- If you could plan a field trip for your class, where would you go?

Social Life

In middle school comes the advent of the cliques. Why do cliques develop? Is your daughter part of a clique? Is she treated fairly by the other students? How can she integrate into this new society?

Stress

How can you tell if your daughter is experiencing stress? Do you know the signs of stress in a youngster? What can you do to help ease your child's stress?

Etcetera

Copyright

All rights reserved. No part of this book may be used or reproduced by any means, graphic, electronic, or mechanical, including photocopying, recording, taping or by any information storage retrieval system without the written permission of the author except in the case of brief quotations embodied in critical articles and reviews.

Disclaimer

The ideas and suggestions in this book are solely the opinion of the author. The author offers no guarantees and holds herself harmless from any and all actions and reactions by following the suggestions located here.

The author of this book does not dispense medical advice or prescribe the use of any technique as a form of treatment for physical, emotional, or medical problems without the advice of a physician, either directly or indirectly. The author's intent is to offer information of a general nature. Should you use any of the information in this book, the author assumes no responsibility for your actions.

This book does not refer to any specific school, teacher, parent, or student and should not be construed as to meaning a particular one unless specifically stated. Any people depicted in stock imagery are models and used for illustrative purposes only.

This handbook is written to assist parents of middle school girls as the girls work their way through the hazards of being a tween. This handbook does not cover extremes of behavior: daughters that never deviate from being a good girl versus girls who get involved with drugs, sex, and/or alcohol. At the first extreme, consider yourself very fortunate. If the second extreme, you need to get professional help for your daughter and a support group for yourself.

Dedication

The effort that went into this book is dedicated to my children, all five who survived middle school and are making a difference in the world. I am so proud of all of them.

I also dedicate this book to teachers and principals who have created a real middle school, one which takes into account the social and emotional growth of these students while meeting the academic goals, no small feat.

About the Author

I earned a doctorate in education, an M.S. and B.S. in elementary education, and Certification as a Public School Administrator. I began my career in education as a teacher of third grade students and later became an elementary school principal, then an elementary and middle school principal. I completed that part of my career as a college professor and head of the education department where I taught prospective teachers.

I reside with my husband and three dogs in our quiet hideaway in the woods of the Pocono Mountains. Together, we raised five children and enjoy four grandchildren.

In my spare time, I love to read and write, and work in my small gift shop. I enjoy traveling and have visited Europe and most of the United States. Publishing an eBook is on my bucket list. I have written three handbooks for parents of kindergarten students, available at www.amazon.com/author/kathleenbenyo.

I am currently working on a book of fiction based upon my experiences as a mother and stepmother as well as a compilation of articles written by my golden retriever, Virginia Jane, previously published locally.

Testing 1-2-3

Below you'll find a short true/false quiz. Take it now before you read the book and then take it again after you've read the book. You might want to have your daughter take the test too. You will gain valuable insight into your tween. At the end of this book are the answers with explanations where required. But refrain from looking back now!

Quiz for Middle School Parents

1. ____ When there's a problem, it's important to tell your child "We need to talk."

2. ____ Middle school is just like high school, only the students are younger.

3. ____If a friend hurts your daughter's feelings, the best thing you can say is "Does it hurt your feelings?"

4. ____Allow your daughter to show when she's angry.

5. ____If your daughter says she hates her hair, offer "Why don't you get your hair cut?"

6. ____It's time to think about college when your daughter starts middle school.

7. ____Negotiate with your daughter.

8. ____Do not allow your daughter to go straight to her room after school; this is a sign of rudeness.

9. ____Your daughter doesn't need to shave in middle school.

10. ____Your daughter is old enough to be left home alone.

11. ____Help your daughter complete her homework.

12. ____Don't encourage extracurricular activities; she'll be busy enough with homework.

13. ____Shop for groceries and pack your daughter's lunch.

14.____Anyone can get a Facebook account.

15.____The most popular method for communicating between tweens is by phone calls.

How Middle Schools Started

For those of us old enough to remember (and I count myself in that group), elementary schools were for grades one through eight, sometimes including kindergarten. Eventually, schools were separated into elementary schools (grades K-6) and secondary schools (grades 7-12).

Junior High School

In the earlier part of the twentieth century, it was seen as disadvantageous to have the oldest students (18 years old) with students barely 13. The junior high school came into being, broken into junior grades 7-9 and secondary grades 10-12. There were some variations on that organization, but that was the basic setup. Grades 7-9 became known as the junior high school. It was a high school but for younger students, so it was named junior. Students changed classes every period, went to lockers, and attended special classes. Teachers were all secondary trained and so the students were treated like miniature high school students.

Middle School

In the mid 1960s, middle schools evolved. It was not a junior high school.

Its purpose was to bridge elementary school and high school. Grades selected were 6-8, with some districts choosing 5-8, 5-9 or 6-9. Both elementary certified and secondary certified teachers could staff a middle school.

Teachers are encouraged to work in groups to ensure the success of all students. One example is when a teacher has a test scheduled for a Tuesday, none of the other teachers schedule a test the same day.

Students are taught how to take notes and how to study, what to highlight and what to concentrate on.

Teachers organize their subject matter with each other. For example, the social studies teacher is teaching his students about inventors and the eras in which they lived. The science teacher can concentrate on what these inventors created and how the inventions work. In Literature (Language Arts/English) class, students can read books about that era or the biographies of the inventors. The topic in art class is also well suited to a social studies lesson and a science lesson experimenting with various art media. That was how middle school was imagined. In some cases, that is not the way it turned out. Your middle school more like a miniature high school? Ask why.

What Is A Tween?

The answers to this question are varied. Some people believe that a tween is someone who has not yet reached their teenage years, so a tween is ages 8-12. Others see a tween as someone in between being a child and being a high school student, so they age them around 11-14. For the purposes of this book, tween is defined as a student aged 11-14.

> *"Be nicer than necessary to everyone you meet. Everyone is fighting some kind of battle."*
>
> --Socrates

Table of Contents

Introduction

Section Summaries

Etcetera

Table of Contents

Behaviors

Bullying

Cell Phones

- Choose, Decide, Pick
- Clothing
- Courses (Examples)
- Curfew
- Clean Your Room!
- Dating
- Doctor and Dentist Visits
- Dangers
- Due Diligence
- Emergency Contact
- Extracurricular Activities
- Home Alone
- Homework
- Internet
- Lunches
- Make up
- Parents' Roles
- Parent/Teacher Conferences
- Prepare Your Child for Middle School

Social Life

Stress

Tattoos

Conclusion

True/False Quiz Answers

Word of Wisdom

Resources

References

Thank You …

Acknowledgements

How to Use This Book

[The remainder of this book has the topics arranged in alphabetical order so you can really use this handbook as a reference book. When there is a footnote, it follows the information provided and is in parenthesis in a smaller font].

> *"The biggest communication problem is we do not listen to understand. We listen to reply."*
> -- Anonymous

Behaviors

Changes in Thinking

Thinking, or cognition, begins to grow for tweens. That's why they think they know everything even though they do not have experience to back up their opinions. They like to argue, and they argue better than they did when they were younger. They think, and they think things through and sometimes come up with some very convincing arguments.

Nancy Darling explains on Psychologytoday.com that tweens are able to think more abstractly, allowing them to create theories and make conclusions. They fit facts to the conclusions they want. Here's a typical conversation:

- Mom, I can't do the dishes. I have too much homework.

- You might have a lot of homework, but doing the dishes is your chore.
- Why is it always my chore?
- Because the other children are too young.
- So I get stuck doing everything and now I won't get my homework done and you'll make me go to bed before I'm finished.
- The dishes will only take fifteen minutes.
- Please let me off the hook just this one time.

- I think you should do the dishes.
- But I only asked this once. It's not like I do it all the time.
- Well ...
- I need a break from doing the dishes every night.
- Maybe ...
- You told me that homework comes first.

She's made her argument and gotten out of doing the dishes. What she failed to mention was that she was texting for almost an hour before dinner when she could have completed some of her homework, still giving her time to do the dishes.

Tweens can tell what your arguments are going to be because they've heard them their entire lives. Now they have enough cognitive and abstract thinking abilities to make good arguments against you. And tweens are relentless. Even if their way of thinking does not make sense, they will stick with it without regard for the absence of facts.

Tweens are developing great logical abilities but they still lack experience to go with them. Hold your ground when your tween starts to argue with you. If it's not a major issue, you might give in (and surprise her!) Or stay the course and the conversation will become her arguing and you answering "No." Don't forget that, just like when they were toddlers, the word No still works and they still know what it means. It's just that they don't like it.

- Can I go to the movies Tuesday night?
- It's a school night and you'll have homework.
- But I'll get it done right after school.
- You'll get home late which means you'll get to bed late and wake up grumpy.
- No, I won't. I promise.

- We have a house rule that, unless it's something unusual, we stay in on school nights.
- That's such a stupid rule! My friends don't have that rule. Can I go?

And so it goes, on and on. Maybe mom can handle it a different way.

- Can I go to the movies Tuesday night?
- No. It's a school night, you have homework, and you have to get to bed at a reasonable time. (you've given an

explanation for your answer).
- But I'll get my homework done right after school.
- No, you may not go.

How does she argue with this? You haven't given her any more ammunition by adding to the argument. She might say, "Why do you have to be so mean?"

You can just walk away.

After she calms down, tell her if she wants to see that movie so badly, she can make plans to go on Friday or Saturday and you'll drive her and her friends to the show.

Inappropriate Language

It's important that she know what the limits are in the house and what she can and cannot say to her parents and her siblings.

If you think she hasn't heard all those four-letter words, think again. She not only has heard them but she may know them. If she hasn't spoken them yet, she has probably used them (or their abbreviations) when texting.

If you want your daughter to use appropriate language, it's vital that you and everyone else in the house use it too. It will become second nature to her to use vulgar language if she hears it at home every day.

Lying

Everyone lies. Sometimes we call them "white lies" or we say we lied to save someone's feelings. But we still lie. Your tween is not lying more than when she was younger, she's just getting better at it.

If you lie, it won't take long for your daughter to notice and when you correct her for lying, the word "Hypocrite" will come out of her mouth. Try to be honest as much as you can. If you make excuses for your lies, your daughter will assume that if she has a good enough excuse, she can get away with lying.

Be sure your daughter feels safe telling the truth at home. Let your child know that you love her no matter what and if she has misbehaved, you will respect her for telling you. There still has to be a consequence for her negative behavior, but you might temper it because she told you the truth and didn't lie.

Try to understand why she is lying. When did the lying start? What triggered it? What does your tween lie about consistently? To whom is she more likely to lie?

Believe your child until you have a reason not to believe her.

Have ongoing conversations about the importance of trust in all kinds of relationships, not just parent and child, but friend-to-friend, girlfriend to boyfriend, teacher to student, and others.

Help your child understand why lying is wrong. "Why am I upset that you lied? How do you feel when you lie to me? When you lie to someone else? When someone lies to you?" (Ed/mag/art/when-teenagers-lie/. Lisa Medoff).

Stealing

You will find very few people who have never taken anything from anyone.

As toddlers, we think that we can just take what another child has because we want it. When we are required to give it back, we cry.

Tweens are somewhat the same. The main reason they steal is because they want something they cannot get on their own. It doesn't have to be anything expensive; price doesn't matter. What matters is how badly she wants it. She may shoplift at a store or steal from her best friend's backpack. When they are found out, they don't want to give it back, claiming it really belongs to them. When they have to give it back, they often cry.

Tweens (and teens) also steal to impress their friends, to add excitement to their lives, to get attention (after all, negative attention is better than no attention), or to feel independent.

(Ed.com/mag/art/when-teenagers-steal. Lisa Medoff).

If you daughter has stolen from a store or another person, she has to give it back or pay for it. She has to admit to the person from whom she stole that she did it. If she doesn't have the money to pay for the item and she's used it (maybe it was as simple as a candy bar), then you'll have to pay for it and she'll have to work off the cost at home by doing extra chores.

Your tween may say to you "How can you do this to me?" or "Why are you embarrassing me like this?" She is pushing the blame for her actions onto you. Don't accept them. She did the stealing. If she is feeling embarrassed, it was her actions that are now causing her to feel this way. You are doing nothing to her except to correct a situation that she handled poorly. It is all on her. Don't let her convince you otherwise.

Don't call your child a thief. She made one mistake. Hopefully, she learned from it. When she is calm, talk about what she's learned from the experience and what she can do to keep it from happening again (especially if she stole in the company of her peers).

Let her know that if it happens again, and you know it won't, there will be more consequences than just repaying or returning. There will be consequences at home and tell her what they will be. Then stick to it. Whether it's not letting her go out for a weekend, or taking away her cell phone for a few days, or giving her extra chores, be sure you select something you will follow through on.

Finally, set a good example. If you borrow something from a neighbor, give it back. Don't steal by accidentally not paying for something in the grocery checkout line. Think of your actions. There may be small actions you do to save a few cents or just for the sake of it, but if you think about your actions, you'll realize you're stealing. That's something you definitely don't want your daughter to learn, especially from you.

Talking Back

Your daughter's brain is growing and she will question decisions or rules more often than when she was younger. So don't be surprised when she starts to question your authority or your rules. If your tween talks back and is disrespectful, here are a few options you can try. (Ed.com/mag/art/when-teens-talk-back. Lisa Medoff)

Some parents give up when their daughter refuses to do what is asked of her. Remember that your daughter does not have control of her impulses like an adult has, and may blurt out a comment she's immediately sorry for but won't apologize or back down. Her brain is still growing.

But that doesn't excuse rude or inappropriate behavior. She has to learn how to control her impulsiveness because her experiences during her tween years help wire her brain to deal with impulses throughout life. So it is important to set clear boundaries. Your daughter needs to know what you will and will not tolerate, and what consequences are incurred for inappropriate behavior.

Make sure your rules are understandable and specific (not general). Be sure she knows what will happen if she breaks the rules.

When your daughter acts inappropriately, stay calm and think before you speak. Do not threaten or yell. This is not the behavior you really want to model. If you or she is getting out of control, end the discussion until you both calm down. Continue the conversation later.

Do not negotiate about the specific rules of the house. Don't let her pull you into a tween argument about the rule or the consequence. If she gets away with the behavior now, it will encourage her to break the rules and to continue to argue about them. Don't waste your time giving a lecture. State your case: here's the rule you broke, here's the consequence. You'll hear "Yes, but …" and it's important that you ignore that last comment.

Talk with your daughter when you're both calm. Discuss the broken rule and if it needs to be adjusted in the future. Listen and discuss, but make your decisions based upon your daughter's safety and well-being.

If your daughter talks back to you, there should be a consequence already in place.

If your daughter uses rude words or comments towards you, let her know that it won't be tolerated. Then tell her that you don't understand what she wants and that you'll listen if she talks about why she is upset. Follow through with the consequence.

"You don't understand!" and "You don't get it!" are overused phrases by tweens. Your response should not be "I've been through it too, you know" or "I certainly understand." You'll get farther if you say, "I don't understand; explain to me what you are feeling." Some professionals believe it is okay for the daughter to respond with a note or by sending an email, but I find that too impersonal. After all is said and done, one-to-one communication is what produces improvements in behavior and better understanding.

Take a minute and think about how you talk to your daughter, your husband, and your other children. Are you modeling rude behavior to your daughter without even realizing it?

If you and your daughter have gotten into the routine of rule breaking and consequences over and over, try to talk with her. Suggest that the two of you do something special together, ask her what she'd like to do, and promise that neither of you will be unkind the entire time you are together. If you're lucky, this may be a turning point.

Show your child the respect you expect. Even when you're angry, it's important for you to step back so you don't start calling her inappropriate names. Telling her she's "no good" or "worthless" may work for you while you're angry but it won't once you calm down. And your daughter certainly won't forget what you said to her.

(Education.com/magazine/art/when-teens-talk-back)

My Story

As each of my five children became adolescents and suffering consequences became necessary, each one responded in a different way. My oldest son didn't care if he were sent to his room. He had no electronics in it, no games to play, but he would read and sleep and rather enjoyed the quiet. So that punishment never worked with him. Keeping him from his friends encouraged his good behavior.

My middle son could live without his friends but don't take away his computer! That was a matter of life and death for him.

My youngest boy was a TV junkie; so taking away TV privileges worked for him.

Both my daughters could not live without the telephone, even though we didn't have cell phones yet.

For each child it's different and also depends upon her age. Study your daughter and find out what really matters to her. If you punish her with something that she doesn't care about, it won't be a punishment.

Point System

One way to handle negative behavior is by removing what she likes and making her earn it back. If you have grounded her and she hates that, then that's what you use to get her attention. If she's always texting, taking away her phone will feel like extreme punishment.

You can choose to use the following format to determine how long the punishment will last. Using this system, your daughter decides how long she will go without something she cares about.

"You have lost the privilege of _____ (going out, using your phone, having friends over, visiting friends, going to a school activity, whatever matters to her).

You must gain _____ (100-250-500) points to regain your privilege."

Now list tasks that she is not normally expected to do. If she sets the table for dinner, don't include that on the list. I saw this suggestion on Facebook (but I don't know to whom to give credit). Here are some examples of what you could include:

- Write a nice letter to someone in the family = 20 points
- Prepare, cook, and serve dinner = 50 points

- Do one load of laundry, not your own (wash, dry, fold, put away) = 100 points
- Empty, clean, and organize one kitchen cupboard = 50 points
- Empty dishwasher = 20 points
- Clean and wash table after dinner = 10 points
- Clean out microwave = 40 points
- Collect and take out all garbage and re-bag all trash cans = 10 points
- Scrub bathroom sink = 10 points
- Clean toilet = 40 points
- Clean bathtub = 25 points
- Water all plants = 25 points
- Straighten and vacuum living room or family room = 40 points

- Sweep and mop kitchen floor = 40 points

Make the point total small for a small offense and large for a more important offense. Let your daughter know in advance that you will be using this system. You can change the system by giving her a list in which every item is worth 10 points (all small jobs) or in which every item is worth 50 points (major tasks). Make sure there are enough for her to make selections. If she has to select 10 to make her quota, make sure you have at least 12 examples.

You may also want to stipulate how often she can do a chore. Emptying the dishwasher is something she can probably do every day, but cleaning the toilet or vacuuming the living room does not need to be done daily.

You can adjust this by the age of the child. You can also switch some of the assignments so the tasks don't get "old".

- Bring down all Christmas decorations from attic = 40 points
- Put away all Christmas ornaments on tree and take to attic = 40 points
- Gather all Christmas decorations, pack, and take to attic = 40 points
- Sweep sidewalk = 20 points
- Shovel snow from sidewalk and steps = 40 points

- Cover all outdoor furniture (or put away) = 30 points
- Walk the dog = 10 points
- Clean up after the dog in the yard = 30 points
- Wash car = 40 points
- Vacuum inside of car, wash windows and dash = 50 points
- Put away groceries = 10 points
- Turn off your cell phone for one day = 40 points
- Stay off computer and iPad for one day = 30 points
- Help your little brother/sister complete their homework/project = 20 points
- Clean the refrigerator, inside and out = 30 points

- Don't watch television (including on computer and iPad) for one day = 30 points

If you find that you are using this method often and that by the time she finishes her points she gets another punishment, then you know this system is not working. Take a break from it.

My Story

I used the point system in the opposite way of how it is described above. I used it as positive reinforcement. My children gained points for a privilege, for example:

- Stay up an hour later
- Have a friend over

- Go to a friend's house
- Have a sleepover
- Call someone long distance (when we had to pay for these charges)
- Go to the bookstore and get a new book
- Go shopping
- Go out to lunch together
- Get an extra thirty minutes on the computer or game system

Whenever the children did more than expected of them, they earned points that they could "turn in" for their special reward.

Think Ahead

You'll have to decide what you will and will not accept from your new middle schooler. What matters? What are you willing to negotiate? What is a solid rule? If your daughter wants to get the latest haircut that you hate, consider if it's such a bad thing. After all, at this age she is not your little clone any more. She is learning to be her own self. Can you put up with a fashionable haircut that is not flattering? Yes, you probably can. However, if she skips doing homework, that is non-negotiable. She must do her homework, all of it.

What will you do if she is always the last person to board the bus? If she is always rushing in the morning? Can you live with that? Probably not, but it's not a major issue as long as she doesn't miss the bus and doesn't forget to take her important items to school. You might want to help her get organized the night before. But it's not the end of the world. What if you find cigarettes in your daughter's backpack? That's a deal breaker. There is no negotiating. Cigarettes are thrown away and you will keep a closer eye on the money she gets and how she spends it. There will be a consequence. Your daughter won't like that decision, but that's why you're the parent.

    Help your daughter think ahead by working together to get her organized. She will have more homework, more projects, and more activities and she may feel overwhelmed. Sometimes, being overwhelmed will cause your daughter to do nothing because she doesn't know where to start. Help her prioritize. Use a calendar. Break large projects into small pieces so that she can do it a little at a time. It won't hurt for you to remind her, without "nagging", of projects she needs to keep ahead of.

Your daughter will need you to support her as she continues on the middle school road. But you'll notice that as she gets older and more accustomed to the rigors of middle school, she will lean on you much less. That's what you want. Well, that's what she needs.

> "By the time a woman realizes her mother was right, she has a daughter who thinks she's wrong."
>
> --Anonymous

Bullying

First of all, let's be sure we know what bullying is. Some parents call every unkind word bullying. But bullying is a very serious event and offense. If another student calls your daughter a name, that is mean and hurtful, but it is not bullying.

Is It Bullying?

Bullying is being mean to the same person over and over. It can include name calling, teasing, threatening, spreading rumors, purposely leaving students out of an event or game, or attacking someone by hitting them or yelling at them. The most important words are "over and over", not just one occurrence.

Bullying doesn't always happen in person. It can occur online or through text messages or emails. The person doing the bullying may post unkind rumors, share embarrassing pictures, or make fake profiles.

"Bullying is aggressive behavior that is intentional, hurtful, and/or threatening and persistent." Bullying includes the following elements:

- Intentional
- Hurtful
- Threatening
- Occurs more than once
- Power imbalance
  (http://bullyfree.com/free-resources/facts-about-bullying)

Physical Bullying Behavior

- Hitting, slapping, slamming, shoving, kicking
- Taking, stealing, damaging or defacing belongings
- Restraining
- Pinching
- Flushing a head into a toilet or pushing someone into their locker
- Throwing food or spitting

Verbal Bullying Behavior

- Name-calling
- Put-downs
- Teasing
- Racist remarks
- Threats

Indirect Bullying

- Turning people against someone
- Destroying reputation
- Humiliation and embarrassment
- Intimidation
- Gossiping, rumors
- Taunting
- Nasty jokes

Cyber Bullying

Negative messages delivered electronically.

Girl Bullies

- Subtle behavior, indirect, sneaky, and nasty.

- Bully other girls in groups.
- Inflict psychological pain more than physical pain.
- Well-behaved around adults.
- Gossip about other girls' sexual behavior.

Is Your Daughter the Bully

Does your daughter bully others? If you see or hear it, intervene immediately and tell her that such behavior will not be tolerated. If she admits that she is only doing it because the other student "started it", tell her to end it. If it's that big of a problem, go to the school or the student's parents. Remain calm. Tell about her experiences. Cooperate. If your daughter is bullying, she may be trying to fit in with the popular kids or think they're better than the kid they're bullying.

There is never a good enough reason for bullying. Students with power use it against those they perceive as having none. They may be bigger, stronger, more popular, smarter, or more attractive. Here are some actions of someone who likes to bully others:

- Seeks to dominate or manipulate others.
- Low tolerance of frustration.
- Has to win at everything; sore "winner" and "loser".
- Gets satisfaction from other's problems or issues.

- Uses others to get what she wants.
- When caught, says the person deserved it.
- Tests authority.
- Breaks class rules.
- Accepts negative attention.
- Has close "followers".

Long Term Problems of a Bullier

- Diabetes and cardiac problems as they age.
- Six times more likely to be convicted of a crime by age 24
- Five times more likely to have a criminal record by age 30.
- May become abusers.
- Excess smoking, drinking, and drug use.

Is Your Daughter Being Bullied

Girls who are bullied often feel different, powerless, unpopular, and very much alone. They think the person doing the bullying is stronger than they are, more popular, and has more friends. They feel like they have no defense.

Bullying can cause a girl to become nervous, feel too sick to go to school, have problems getting along with others at school or getting poor grades, or may turn around and bully other kids just to feel powerful again. Some signs that your daughter may be being bullied:

- Skipping school.

- Poor academic performance.
- Easily distracted.
- Wants to go a different way to school or doesn't want to ride the bus.
- Lack of interest is school activities.
- Body Image: hunches shoulders, hangs head, won't look people in the eye.
- Prefers adults to other students.
- Frequent real or fake illnesses.
- Stammer or stutter develops suddenly.
- Quick-tempered.
- Cautious, clingy, nervous, anxious, fearful.
- Frequently asks for extra money.
- Possessions are often "lost".

- Starts bullying siblings or other children.
- Aggressive and rebellious.
- No respect for authority.
- Talks about or attempts suicide.
- Cuts self, overeats or refuses to eat.
- Drastic change in appearance.

Practice

Although your daughter may initially think you're silly, take the time to practice what she can do if someone bullies her by calling her names or teasing her (or whatever else you think you should do).

Help her not to accept the mean comments. Let her know that she is more than the girls who are teasing her; she is a better person than they are. Let her practice walking away while saying to herself "That's not me" or "She doesn't know what she's talking about" or "She's just jealous" or simply repeat, "I don't care".

Encourage her to talk with you about any bullying she experiences or sees.

If Your Daughter Sees Bullying

Seeing such behavior may make her scared that if she says anything, she will be bullied too. She may want to stay home from school because she doesn't feel safe there. The best thing she can do is report the bullying to an adult who can stop the bullying. Unfortunately, most tweens do not believe that adults are very helpful when bullying is reported to them.

Facts About Bullying

- Over 3.2 million students are victims of bullying each year.
- About 160,000 teens skip school every day because of bullying.
- Seventeen per cent of students report being bullied 2-3 times a month or more.
- Seventy-one per cent of students report bullying as a problem at their school.

- Seventy-four per cent of eight to eleven year olds said teasing and bullying occur at their schools.
- Every seven minutes, a child on an elementary playground is bullied.
- Ninety per cent of fourth through eighth graders report being victims of bullying (90%!).
- Thirty per cent of all child suicides are directly related to bullying.
- Physical bullying increases in elementary school, peaks in middle school, and declines in high school. Verbal abuse remains constant.

  (https://www.dosomething.org/facts/11-facts-about-bullying).

When and Where Is Bullying'

Bullying begins around age three or four. It happens more often in school than on the school bus, believe it or not. It occurs where there is little or no adult supervision. It occurs everywhere, in all kinds of schools and in many countries.

Problems Caused by Bullying

- Criminal cases.
- Lawsuits.
- Fearful school climate.
- Common theme in school shootings; the shooters usually have been bullied.
- Stress.
- Runaways.

- Suicide risk, even in bystanders.
- Gang membership to feel they belong.
- Teen pregnancies to have someone to love and be loved.
- Dropouts.
- School absence.
- Poor academic performance.

For the full report on bullying, go to http://bullyfree.com/free-resources/facts-about-bullying

> *"I've never run into a person who yearns for their middle school days."*
>
> --Jeff Kinney

Cell Phones

Text messaging is the most popular method teens (and tweens) use to communicate with each other. The most frequent users of text messaging are youngsters from 13-17 years old. Seventy-two per cent of all teens use text messaging, more than use the phone for voice conversation or talking face-to-face. Email has dropped in popularity for tweens while Twitter.com has become more popular.

(file://localhost/(http/::www.cdc.gov:std:life-stages-populations:Adolescents-white-paper.pdf).

    Should you have access to your tweens' texts? There are no easy answers to that question. Tweens don't think parents should be permitted to read their texts. They compare that to reading a diary. Parents, on the other hand, believe they should have access to texts, even if they don't read them every day. Parents' point of view is that this is the best way to keep track of what's going on in their daughter's life. They also point out that they are paying the phone bill.

From my point of view, I think kids should know that their parents retain the right to review their texts on occasion. By doing so, if there is nothing that leads to concern, you can check less often. Show your daughter that you trust her once she's gained your trust.

"... school sucked. It was a universal truth
(that) whoever said these were supposed to be
the best years of your life
was probably drunk
or delusional."

-- Kami Garcia and Margaret Stohl

Choose, Decide, Pick

From "How to Talk to Your Middle Schooler" by Chuck Moorman, these three words are necessary for you to help your child add to her vocabulary.

Tweens tend to not want to take responsibility for their actions. They are quick to blame others. "That teacher gave me a bad grade" instead of "I really didn't study for the test" and "Julie got me in trouble" instead of "I got in trouble" and how about "That teacher is so mean to me" try "I'm rude to that teacher."

"If you *choose* to let your clothes on the bedroom floor, you won't have anything clean or neat to wear."

"If you *decide* to talk back to your father, you'll have to stay home Friday night."

"If you *pick* rude friends, you're going to be seen as one of them."

You can help them learn the importance of choosing, deciding, and picking.

"If you *choose* to get your laundry done, we can pick up your friend and go out for lunch."

"If you *decide* to rake all the leaves, you can have the rest of the day to yourself."

"If you *pick* practicing over talking on the phone, you might make the team."

These three words help tweens learn that they have some control over their lives, that what happens to them is not caused by someone else, and that they need to take responsibility for their actions.

Try using these words when you talk to your daughter. Eventually, you will be surprised at her positive responses to what you say (still after the grumbling).

"It's well known that many girls have a tendency to dumb down when they're in middle school."

--Sally Ride

Clothing

Keep in mind that your daughter will probably go through a growth spurt during middle school and all the cute clothes you bought her at the start of school won't fit any more. Set a reasonable budget for clothing; do not include shoes, boots, or sneakers. Do include underwear and pantyhose or leggings. Sit with your daughter and develop a list of absolutely needed items after checking the school's website for their dress policy. Their policy may severely limit your choices. If there is not a specific, detailed dress policy, stay with pieces that can be worn with other pieces to make new outfits: jeans, slacks, skirts, blouses, shirts, tops, and sweaters. Use what she had from the year before that still fit and cross them off the list. Keep reminding her of the budget. Encourage the purchase of machine wash and dry clothing.

If she insists that she wants or needs expensive sneakers like everyone else is wearing, and it doesn't fit into your budget, she can earn them by doing extra chores around the house, babysitting, running errands for neighbors, caring for plants and gardens, or walking dogs. If she wants something badly enough, she'll find a way to make money. You can make her a deal that, however much she makes, you'll match it. That will encourage her and make the goal seem closer.

Sometimes you'll just have to tell her that something is out of the question because of price. I have a friend who just bought her son a pair of $200 sneakers for school because he "just had to have them." Now she doesn't have the money to buy new clothes for him. She explained to him that she will get him a few items, but mostly he'll have to wear what fits from last year because he spent his budget on the sneakers. I'm not sure he understands why he still can't have new clothes along with the sneakers.

Do Some Surveillance

Park at a school bus stop and pay attention to the older girls as they arrive for school or are dropped off after school. What are they wearing? What kind of shoes? Are they carrying backpacks? Lunch sacks? Attend a middle school function and watch the students. Talk to their parents and learn from them. They'll be too happy to share where the quicksand is.

When looking for clothes, don't forget about yard sales and flea markets. You don't need to purchase an entire wardrobe this way, but you might find three or four very nice pieces for just a few dollars. The Salvation Army and thrift shops are other places to browse. If you think your daughter would be offended by having clothes that have been worn, don't tell her. This is one time you just come home with a few pieces that you found on sale. And that's true. Just be sure you select sweaters that are not pilled, or clothes with stains or tears or missing buttons. Be extremely picky when you shop at these locations, keeping in the front of your mind what girls are wearing.

Laundry

While discussing budgets and clothing, tell your daughter that she will be doing her own laundry and you will teach her. Show her how to run the washer and dryer, how many items to put in at a time, which pieces of lingerie need to be washed inside a lingerie bag, and what colors go together. Show her how much detergent and fabric softener to use, and that fabric softener is never used on towels. Her towels should be washed at least weekly, the same as her bed linens. The first few times she does her own laundry, help her separate her clothing.

Teach her that as soon as the dryer is finished, she needs to remove the pieces and either fold them or put them on hangers or she'll have even more work to do ironing pieces that didn't need to be ironed. By letting her clothes in the washer or dryer, she is keeping other family members from doing their laundry. Help her decide what pieces are clean and just need to be put away, not washed. Explain that the more often a piece of clothing is washed, the less new it looks and it often loses its color and becomes dull.

"School is learning things you don't want to know, surrounded by people you wish you didn't know, while working toward a future you don't know will ever come."

-- Dave Kellett

Courses (Examples)

Math, Sixth Grade

By this time, the teacher expects your daughter to know the four basic math operations (addition, subtraction, multiplication, and division) as well as fractions, percentages, decimals, and basic graphing. She should be a little familiar with formulas for perimeter and area of basic shapes. You can go online and Google "[your state] core curriculum math" to get specific information about what to expect, not only in sixth grade, but also in seventh and eighth.

Your child will be introduced to algebra. You can help by giving her questions that are really algebraic equations. "We're going to visit grandma on Sunday. She lives 20 miles away and we'll be traveling 40 miles an hour. How long will it take us to get there? If we leave at 10:00, what time shall I tell grandma that we'll be there?"

In geometry, your child will work with three-dimensional shapes.

They'll interact with statistics and probability when they'll have fun rolling die and tossing coins.

There'll be a lot of word problems. For some, your daughter won't have to solve the problem, she'll have to write about what methods she would use to

solve the problem. Memorization of facts gives way to using those facts for thinking critically.
(Education.com/magazine/article/sixth_grade_math).

Social Studies in Seventh Grade

Your child has made it through the first year of middle school. What will she learn in Social Studies this year? Again, Google the information for your state. There is usually a focus on world history and the rise of Europe. There may also be state history. There will be a focus on geography, and relationships between people and the lands they settled.

Your child will come across new vocabulary terms and concepts such as various religions, the Renaissance and Enlightenment.

Regardless of the topic, the National Council of Social Studies Teachers wants students to do more than memorize – to learn. You can help by talking about your own experiences, news, leaders, and more. Your child is developing higher-level thinking, so listen when they share their own ideas.

If you find out that your child will be studying your state's history, make plans to go on your own field trips to some of the historic locations within your reach.

Your daughter will have more projects to do – and regardless what other parents do, it is her assignment, not yours. You can help her by breaking a project down into its parts, printing each part on a sticky note that you place on the back of her bedroom door or other convenient location. Teach her that she can work on one part at a time, which will cause less stress than trying to do it all at once.

You can also help by making sure she has all of the materials she needs for the project (poster board, markers, glue, scissors, and other items to complete the project). Then encourage her and support her while *she* does the work.

> *"The butterflies in my stomach turn into vampire bats as we pull up to the school."*
> ☐ Cat Clarke, *Torn*

Curfew

It's a dirty word for many tweens. They want to be treated as adults and be allowed to stay out as long as their friends do. In the summer, it is reasonable to allow her to be out until 8-9PM. But that depends upon who she's with and where she is. Those are facts you need to know at all times. If her plans change, you need to know. If the kids she's hanging out with change, you need to know.

Tell her that if she doesn't keep you updated, you will come and get her and take her home, regardless of what time it is (and how embarrassing it may be for her). If you can't find her, and she finally saunters home, without malice tell her that she is not going anywhere the next night. All of this leads to the need for her to have a cell phone, but we'll get to that later.

School Nights

On school nights, curfew should be at 7PM, maybe a little later for eighth graders. And that means she's done her homework, helped with dinner, ate with her family, and cleaned up after dinner. That may not leave her much time. If she finishes homework early or has no homework, you can allow her to go out for an hour before dinner. But she must be home to eat dinner with the family.

Weekends

On weekends, curfew for a sixth grader is usually around 8:30PM, and 9:00PM for seventh and eighth graders. Or you could give your eighth grader that extra half hour until 9:30PM. Again, you want to know where she is and with whom.

In the Evening

Your daughter needs about thirty minutes to transition from her very busy lifestyle to a more quiet one at home. This is a good time for her to pack her backpack and her lunch, check the schedule on the refrigerator to make sure there's not anything extra she needs for the next day. If she likes to shower in the evening, that would be the next event. You decide when the cell phone gets turned off, but not later than thirty minutes before lights out. Make her bring her phone downstairs, turn it off, and put it in the recharger until the morning.

Be Firm

Be firm about your curfew. Don't deviate or it won't be long before your child will deviate too. If she is visiting at someone's home, there should be adult supervision or she should not stay. If she's going to be late, she must call and report that she'll be late and by how long. Listen to her excuse, don't lose your temper. Tell her that to make up for the time she was late today, she will give up that much time tomorrow or the next time she goes out. If her curfew is 8:30PM and she arrives home at 9, that's thirty minutes late. The next time she goes out she has to be in by 8PM to make up for those thirty minutes. When she knows you mean it and will follow through, she will follow these rules.

Remember, you are criticizing the *actions* of your daughter; you are not criticizing your *daughter*. Instead of "Why are you always late?" or "Why can't you do what you're told?" try "You know what time your curfew is and you'll have to make up the time the next time you want to go out." This doesn't mean she won't kick her feet and throw a mini-tantrum. She may even try to engage you in an argument. Stand firm but fair. She knows it all makes sense and that you're not finding fault with her.

But ...

Keep in mind that all rules have exceptions. If your child attends a school dance, is on the basketball team or is a cheerleader, chances are the ending of the event will override the curfew. In that case, pick up your child when it's over or give her fifteen minutes to get home once the event ends.

Kids say, "Curfews were meant to be broken" while adults say, "Curfews were meant to be followed."

Good Night!

Be sure she gets enough sleep. Middle school students should average 9 hours of sleep a night but that is tough to ensure. If your child has to get up at 6AM, she'd have to be in bed with lights out by 9PM and sometimes that is not feasible.

Schools tend to do things backwards. Young children, as you know, are up early every morning, often watching cartoons and having a snack. Their circadian rhythm enables them to wake up early. But when do they go to school? Often, after all the middle school and high school students have been delivered to school.

On the other hand, middle school students are only too happy to stay in bed on the weekends. You usually have to drag them from their beds before noon. They need that extra sleep, yet they have to be in school early. Schools should switch it around! Send the little ones in first and home first, and have the older ones start later and stay later. But that won't happen so this is the end of my rant.

When she goes to bed, the cell phone comes downstairs and gets plugged into the charger until the morning. No laptop or computer is in her room either. It won't make you popular but it will keep your child safe.

The 9-hour plan should be followed on weekends too. Let your child stay up later (maybe until 10PM). Waken her around 8AM. A little over 9 hours, but close enough. If she sleeps for 12 hours on weekend nights, rolling out of bed at noon, she will have a much more difficult time getting up in the morning for school.

Allow her to wake up slowly, and then have breakfast.

After that, it's time for chores. She should completely empty her backpack: that means, take everything out of it. Wipe out the bottom and pockets of the backpack. Then repack, throw away unnecessary papers, hand paperwork to you. She can do the same with her lunch sack, if she uses one. Now would be a good time for her to do her laundry. Do the bed linens first so she can put them right back on the bed. Then her laundry, and finally her towels which can be washed with the family towels. Your daughter can clean up her bedroom and help with chores around the house and still be finished by noon.

> *"The biggest communication problem is we do not listen to understand. We listen to reply."*
> -- Anonymous

Clean Your Room!

You may send your daughter to her room to clean up, and when you check on her a half hour later, she's still sitting on her bed in the middle of her mess. Before you lose your patience, consider that she doesn't know how to "straighten" her room. Now is a teachable moment, a little at a time. First, help her decide what to do with all the clothes lying around. Wash? Hang back up? Never wear again? Needs repair?

Demonstrate how to separate laundry from the clothes to hang up. Are they dirty? Terribly wrinkled? They all need to be washed. Underwear that's only been worn once always needs to be washed. She can then take over with creating a pile of laundry and hanging up her clothes. Does she know how to put on a fitted sheet? After they're washed and dried, you may need to show her.

While her clothes are washing and drying, she can sweep or vacuum her room, dust, and put things away that don't have a home. When you work at her closet, make space on the floor for her shoes.

Once she's finished her laundry, she has the rest of the day (unless she has to help with or clean up after lunch). She will quickly discover that she wants to hang her clothes up after wearing them so she doesn't have to go through the time it takes to wash and dry them. And then have to put them away anyway!

She may want to take it easy, use the computer, talk on the phone, visit a friend or have a friend visit her. She can work on a project or complete homework, although many students prefer to do weekend homework on Sunday evenings, as it gets their mindset ready for school the next day.

Although you have a million chores to do, try to find time to spend with your daughter during the weekend. These times are priceless, whether it's shopping, watching a movie on TV together, or enjoying ice cream. You may learn more about your daughter's life during these occasions than when you ask questions directly.

> *"I started cooking out of middle school depression."*
>
> --Zac Posen

Dating

This is a major topic that I approach separately; it could and does take up pages and pages of information, suggestions, and hopefully solutions. My input on dating and sexual activity can be found in my soon to be released book for parents of middle school girls called <u>Not My Daughter: Middle School Dating and Sex</u>. It includes valuable information on these topics as well as other looming issues for young girls. It offers details on how they impact the ability of a middle school girl to think and make choices. The book provides the very latest research on their effects.

Doctor and Dentist Visits

If you child is due for her regular checkups, plan ahead. Schedule the appointments for the summer, before school starts. That way she won't miss school time.

Immunizations

Ask your doctor. Be sure your daughter has all other necessary immunizations. If you're unsure, check your school's website, call the school, or ask your doctor. Most middle schoolers are required to have a tetanus diphtheria vaccine (Tdap) for entry to middle school. This would be the perfect time for your daughter to get the first dose of the HPV vaccine and meningococcal vaccines.

Dangers

If you think your daughter is not going to be exposed to drugs, alcohol, or cigarettes, it's time for you to think again. Use of drugs and alcohol is prevalent for tweens and some tweens consider it a rite of passage: if you don't do it, we'll throw you out of the group, we'll make fun of you, you won't have any friends. Girls are afraid of being ostracized by the very group to which they want to belong.

As for drugs, it was evident in my school too. One young man went to the bathroom every day regardless of what class he was in. So we compared sign-out sheets for bathroom use and found that yes, he was asking to use the bathroom at the same time every afternoon. Interestingly, we discovered that another boy asked to use the bathroom every day about ten minutes after the first boy. It was too much time for them to be together in the bathroom, so what was going on? I researched the issue by entering the boys' bathroom after the first boy used it and the bathroom was empty. It took some searching, but I found a stash taped to the bottom of one of the sinks. The second boy picked it up every day. I wrote a note that said, "You're caught!" and taped it under the sink. Ten minutes later the second boy used the bathroom and came out looking quite startled. He ended up in my office where he admitted the ploy and the first boy joined him there with all the parents. They're had been clever – for a while.

Most Popular Drugs

The most widely used drugs by middle school students are marijuana followed by prescription medicine (not prescribed for them). (http://www.drugabuse.gov/publications/media-guide/commonly-abused-drugs). In 2013, seven per cent of eighth graders use marijuana occasionally every month and a smaller percentage use marijuana every day. Because marijuana is being decriminalized, kids think it's safe. (http://www.drugabuse.gov/publications/drugfacts/high-school-youth-trends). Fewer teens smoke cigarettes than smoke marijuana.

Tweens and teens said that they use prescription drugs, in particular Adderall, Vicodin, cough medicine, and tranquilizers. As for inhalants, about five per cent of eighth graders report using them.

About three percent of eighth graders admitted to getting drunk. One quarter of adolescents (includes high school students) reported using alcohol and twenty per cent used an illicit drug.

A study of youths aged 12 to 17 was made and provides the following results, as of that year: seven per cent were current users of marijuana, three percent used prescription drugs, one percent used inhalants, and less than one percent were users of cocaine.

Among tweens 12 to 13 years old, two percent used prescription drugs and one percent used marijuana. Among children 14 to 15 years old, six percent used marijuana, and 2.5 percent used prescription drugs. The percentages aren't high but show an increase in use as the children get a year or two older.

The use of currently illicit drug use was almost ten percent. For tween/teen girls, use of marijuana was about seven percent. Among persons aged 12 or older, the rate of current illicit drug use in the eastern United States was almost ten percent. That's one in ten adolescents. Of those who use marijuana, seventeen percent use it daily.

(http://samhsa.gov/data/NSDUH/2012SummNatFindDetTables/NationalFindings/NSDUHresults2012.htm#fig2.8).

For students who smoke cigarettes, the rate of illicit drug use was higher than for non smokers. Additionally, among youths age 12-17 who were heavy drinkers, they also used drugs and tobacco. Drug use among students who smoke cigarettes and drink alcohol was almost 69%.

There are a lot of figures here, but what this shows is that if a student is involved in one of these three negative activities, the chances that she will engage in the other one or two is greater, much greater. Students who engage in these dangerous activities are also more likely to become sexually active.

For students who used prescription drugs of any kind, more than fifty percent of them got the drugs for free from a friend or relative. About twenty percent had their own prescription, ten percent bought them from a friend or relative, and four percent stole them from a friend or relative.

Keep your prescription medications in a safe place

The bathroom is one of the worst places to keep drugs because the moisture in the room may affect the effectiveness of the drug or even soften the pills. They are also in a perfect location for your child to help herself to these drugs, if not for herself, maybe for a friend or to sell them. Keep your medications together in a container in your bedroom where it is more difficult for your child to get to them. I know some parents who keep their medications in a lock box.

Count your pills. It is your job to keep track of your medicines. If you discover that some are missing, move their location and be more vigilant. If you feel the need, keep a small note pad with your medications and note when you take them. Not only will you keep better track, but if your daughter knows that you have a record of how many you have, she will be less inclined to take them.

Alcohol Use

First, let's define the terms for this section.

- Current use (taken within the past month when the study was done): at least one drink
- Binge use: five or more drinks on the same occasion
- Heavy use: five or more drinks on the same occasion on each of five or more days within thirty days.

A little more than half of adolescent reported being current drinkers. Almost twenty-five percent of these adolescents were binge drinkers, and about 6.5 percent were heavy drinkers.

For children aged 12-13, use of alcohol was about 2 percent. When children reach ages 14-15, the use soars to 11 percent. It jumps to 25 percent for students ages 16-

17! Binge drinking among 12-13 year olds was one percent but for 14-15 year olds was 5.5 percent. The area with the most student drinkers occurs in northeastern United States.

Do not offer alcoholic beverages to your daughter, even during a holiday celebration. You are telling her that alcohol is okay. If you, yourself, are a binge drinker, you need to take a long, hard look at yourself and consider what your behavior is doing to your daughter and how it is influencing her.

My Story

When I was a middle school principal, we had a problem with kids bringing vodka to school in water bottles. It has no smell and it's clear, so it is difficult to discover. We also found vodka in 7-Up and other bottles from clear liquids. We did discover that it was happening even with the "good" kids. It was "the thing" to do. We ruled that any bottled water brought to school had to have a sealed cap. That solved our problem, for the most part.

We also found out that kids who walked to school carried vodka and water and hid the bottles on the way to school so they could retrieve them on the way home. We alerted parents and did our due diligence but tweens can be very conniving. We were told about a Halloween party where one of the boys spiked the punch, but we could never prove it.

Never host a party for your daughter and her friends and offer alcohol of any kind. Not only are you sending the wrong message, but also you could be held legally responsible.

Tell your daughter not to stay at a party where alcohol is provided. She can call you for a ride home, no questions asked. She needs to stand up for herself and display her self-respect.

Cigarette Smoking

About 26 per cent of adolescents aged 12-17 smoke cigarettes; that's one in four students, a large number. Tobacco is an addictive drug that causes many diseases as a person ages as well as decreasing life span. Getting off cigarettes is difficult, so the sooner she does it, the better.

If you smoke in front of your daughter, think twice. You are her role model and she won't understand why she can't smoke while you do. Further, second hand smoke is dangerous to her.

Remember, if she smokes she is more likely to try something else, especially marijuana.

It is your right and responsibility to check her room if you suspect she has cigarettes, drugs, or alcohol. Look for matches, lighters, small plastic bags of what looks like oregano or more serious, a very small bag with a white powder. If she keeps soda bottles in her room, it would not be unreasonable if they are open for you to taste them.

> " ... My middle school experience was ... horrible. I got picked on like no tomorrow."
>
> --Zachary Levi

Due Diligence

Be the Chauffer

One of the best ways to keep track of your daughter's activities and friends is to offer to be the driver to take them to the movies, the mall, or a school activity.

Listen closely but don't interrupt. You'll be surprised at how much you'll learn once the girls are used to you. They forget that you're even there.

Volunteer

With the little bit of spare time you can find, volunteer in the school. One good place is the library, where you can assist students in finding material they need. You'll learn a lot about the teachers this way too!

Attend Meetings

If daytime is not possible, attend PTA or PTO meetings and volunteer to chaperone school dances. Your daughter may cringe at the thought of you serving as a chaperone, but she'll get over it. If you can get a day off work, volunteer to chaperone a field trip, field day, or another event at school. You don't have to tie yourself to a weekly obligation, but once in a while will help you keep your pulse on your daughter and her friends.

> *"It's easier to floss with barbed wire than admit you like someone in middle school."*
> -- Laurie Halse Anderson, *Speak*

Emergency Contact

Choosing an emergency contact is often the last thing parents think about. They just write down a name and phone number and forget about it. But there's some criteria related to choosing an emergency contact.

First of all, it should be someone who knows your daughter and who your daughter knows. If an emergency contact has to pick her up at school because she is ill or injured, the last thing you want is to have a stranger arrive at the school.

The emergency contact should know a little about your daughter. She should know of any medications she takes regularly and anything to which she has an allergy or reaction. Sometimes things are missed in school, and the emergency contact can be prepared to offer information they may not otherwise have.

This is pretty obvious, but your emergency contact should not work with you. If there's a reason you can't get your daughter, your emergency contact might have the same reason.

Choose someone you know can handle an emergency phone call, who won't be overwhelmed by it.

Your emergency contact should have a copy of the medical insurance card that covers your daughter, in the event she has to go to the hospital. You might also give your emergency contact a well-phrased, professionally written or typed permission for that person to sign for emergency services for your daughter.

"In my absence, I, _____(parent's name), parent of _____ (daughter's name), date of birth _____ give permission for our emergency contact person, _____ (their name), to sign for any and all medical services necessary for my daughter.

This permission is in effect from September 1, 2015 until June 1, 2016.

Signature and Date: _____ _____"

    Give the original statement to your emergency contact and retain a copy for yourself. You may also want to provide the school nurse and classroom/homeroom teacher with a copy.

When you make a copy of your medical insurance card for your emergency contact person, underneath the copy of the card write the names and dosages of medications your daughter takes regularly, any allergies, and any negative reactions she's had to anything, including foods, insects, medications, and anything else that cause her to have a negative reaction. Then write down all of the phone numbers at which you might be reached and include an email address.

Provide at least two phone numbers for your emergency contact, if at all possible. If one is a cell phone, note that so the school knows they can also use text messages to contact her. Provide her email address also.

If you change your emergency contact person, inform the school as soon as possible. Thank the former emergency contact person for their assistance and let them know that their services will no longer be needed (if they don't already know). Then give all of the necessary information to the new contact person.

Chances are slim that your emergency contact will ever need to use these documents, but it's good to have them. She should keep them in a safe place that she can access quickly in the event she gets a phone call from the school.

Extracurricular Activities

Your daughter will be offered more options than ever before. There will be clubs she can join, teams she can try out for, and service activities within the school.

Talk to your daughter in advance of these decisions. What is she interested in? What is she good at or would like to improve? How often does this group meet? Is it a club that meets once a week after school or a daily practice routine like basketball? What does she have time for? How much does it cost? Can you afford it? Is there a small membership fee or are there particular sneakers she has to have? What if she joins or is accepted and doesn't like it? Does she have to stick it out or can she "unjoin" (instead of quit, which sounds so negative).

What will you both do if it's a team sport and she's cut? How will you handle that? Of course you will not blame her or find fault. Maybe the team needs an equipment manager or a student scorekeeper. Maybe she can be part of the team that way. If not, she need not ignore the sport. Encourage her to attend some of the games and cheer on her classmates. She'll be seen as a team player, even if she's not on the team. Maybe she can find someone to work with her to improve her skills before tryouts the following year.

Talk this out, maybe over a few days rather than all at once. Maybe she'd like to do a school activity like student council or tutoring younger children.

Keep in mind that your child can't join everything! Even middle schoolers, especially girls, suffer from stress and fatigue. If they are constantly running from homework to practice, stuffing down some food along the way, not getting enough sleep and waking up cranky, this all can be signs of stress and fatigue. It may be time to cut back or reconsider options. At the very least, drop an email to your child's homeroom teacher or coach and ask his opinion or if you can meet with him to discuss her schedule.

My Story

One of my sons joined a baseball team. He went faithfully to practice. He never got to play. He became disgruntled and wanted to quit. I said he had to stay with it because he chose to join. His father advised me to find out a little more about the activity. So, for a few days, when I dropped him off for practice, I stayed in my car and watched. My son and another boy were given a ball and told to go to the outfield (by the homerun fence) and throw the ball to each other. Was this to improve his skills? No. Not one coach or assistant spoke to these two boys throughout the entire practice and they were not included in the drills and skill practice with the rest of the team. It was clear to me that their coach had decided they weren't worth his time or effort and had, in a sense, banned him from practice. I allowed my son to quit (unjoin) that day. Neither he nor I ever regretted that decision.

> *"I'll be famous one day, but for now I'm stuck in middle school with a bunch of morons."*
> -- Jeff Kinney, *Diary of a Wimpy Kid*

Home Alone

This is among the most difficult decisions a parent has to make. There is a big difference between being home alone for thirty minutes while you run an errand and coming home to an empty house and letting themselves in (latchkey child).

The age of 10 is commonly accepted as the youngest age at which a child can be left home alone. But that doesn't mean all ten-year-olds are ready or capable of being left home alone.

We'll start with the bottom line: if you're not sure, chances are your child is not ready.

When you do feel the time has come, begin with practice. Arrange to go out for about thirty minutes during daytime when your child is already home. Call after ten minutes to ask how she is doing. Be home within the thirty minutes you promised. If, when you get home, she seems flustered or uncomfortable, she's not ready.

It's one thing to let your daughter home alone, but it's a totally different story when she has younger siblings to care for. Then you need to consider them and how well they follow the house rules. You'll have to talk with the younger children so they know your daughter is in charge and they must listen to her. I suggest that when you begin with home without a parent that she's home alone with no one else to care for.

Post a list of phone numbers where she can easily find them. Include your work number, your cell phone number, the phone number of a trusted neighbor, and 911. If a child gets really scared, she may forget 911.

Be sure your daughter knows where the fire extinguisher is and how to use it and when. The first rule when there is a fire is to get out of the house and then call 911.

Your daughter should know where the first aid kit is (primarily for Band-Aids).

Can your daughter tell time (using a regular clock)? It might sound like a silly question but she may need to know what time you'll be home and be able to calculate what time it will be in thirty minutes. Even using a digital clock, she needs to be able to calculate future times.

Remind her not to open the door to anyone except for her parents (who might come home separately). Mom may have left her home alone but dad may arrive home first. She must be sure who it is before she even thinks of opening the door. If she's not sure, the door stays locked. This may be an inconvenience for dad, but it's better that she follow safety rules.

Will you allow her to answer the phone (or her own phone) while you are gone? If so, stress that she must not tell anyone that she is home alone, including her best friend. If someone comes to the door, she does not need to respond to whoever is there and they will leave.

If your daughter becomes uncomfortable or ill at ease, she should call you immediately.

When she's comfortable being alone for thirty minutes during the day, go for sixty minutes during daylight. Then go for thirty minutes at night, then sixty minutes. After all these times, both you and she will know if she's able to be home alone or home with her younger siblings.

Practice. Leave the house and knock on the door. Have her make believe it's a stranger. What does she do? Be insistent about being let in (my car broke down, for example). Practice having her answer the phone. What does she say if someone wants to speak with you? How does she handle that without saying that she's home alone? Practice having her call 911, giving her full name and address. You can ask her some questions as if you were the operator on the other end of the line. These practices are worthwhile, even though your daughter may think they are silly.

Some simple rules to follow

- Do not use the stove, oven, toaster, or iron.
- Have a snack that doesn't need to be warmed (like yogurt).

- In case of fire, leave the house immediately and then call 911.
- Do not leave the house unless there's a fire.
- Work on homework.
- Do not unlock the door or open a window for any reason.
- Complete chores (if you've left a list).
- Do not touch matches or a lighter for any reason.
- No friends may visit.
- Don't tell anyone that you are alone.

She should know where to find emergency lighting in the event of a power outage (at least one flashlight that works). It's also helpful to have some battery-operated candles that she can use to light up a room.

Make certain that all firearms are locked away and she has no way to get the key.

If your daughter will be home alone for a large part of the day (if you have to work), make a list of chores for her to do. She may not like it, but it will keep her busy and help to pass the time. Check in frequently.

Praise her when you get home for how well she handled herself (and her siblings) while you were gone. Let her know your trust in her has grown and you appreciate that she followed all the rules.

You don't want to let your child home alone very often. It should be the exception, not the rule.

Homework

The increase in homework from elementary school to middle school is dramatic. Your daughter may feel completely overwhelmed, causing nothing to get done. You can't and shouldn't do your child's homework for her, but you can help her become more organized which will make doing homework less of a chore.

Materials

Be sure she has all the "equipment" she needs to complete her job (homework). Ensure she has pencils, a sharpener, pens, highlighters, colored pencils, crayons, rulers, calculator, paper (both lined and unlined), sticky notes, stapler and staples, paper clips, and a kitchen timer.

Calendar

Print out pages of a calendar from the Internet. Together, mark when certain assignments are due. To keep current, do this every day. She will soon be able to do this without your help. If she has a long term project that isn't due for weeks, mark when it is due and then mark dates before the due date ("Science project due in two weeks!"). Or have her break the large assignment into parts that are marked on the calendar along the way (outline map for project; fill in names of countries; color each country).

Lists

Your daughter can also, with your assistance, make a list of things that need to be done in one week. She can include school work, after school activities, church functions, time with friends. When she sees all that she expects to complete in one week, it's time to prioritize! She can list all of the activities in their order of importance. Or she can separate the items into groups A, B, C. A = must be completed this week. B = should be completed if time. C = only if extra time is available.

Timer

Use a kitchen timer; it will actually reduce stress. Your daughter may estimate how much time it will take her to do each activity or homework project. If she allows herself 20 minutes to complete the project, she can set the timer at 18 minutes so she knows that she's almost out of time. If she finishes early and has checked her work, then she has a few free minutes for a quick phone call, snack, or just relaxing time. If it takes her the full 20 minutes (or more), she should still give herself 5 minutes of rest time before tackling the next assignment. She should get up and walk around, get something to drink, call a friend, or use the bathroom. If she stays sitting where she works, she's not rewiring herself to start again. Especially with reading assignments, this short break will renew her attention.

> *"Those who are hardest to love need it the most."*
> -- Socrates

Internet

Use of the Internet could be an entire book by itself. There's so much good and, unfortunately, so much bad regarding the Internet.

Where to Place the Computer

Let's start by reminding you not to place the computer in an isolated location. It should be where it's not too noisy, but where you can easily stop and look over her shoulder. If she doesn't like you doing that, she has the choice of not using the computer at all.

Electronics at Bedtime

If you have made the decision to allow her to have her laptop or iPad in her bedroom, think twice about that. Problems online are more likely to occur in the privacy of one's own room. At the very least, require that all electronics be brought downstairs at bedtime. Keep the charger downstairs too. This is a tough time to be a parent!

To avoid only negative comments about the Internet, start by explaining and reviewing house rules for the Internet. These house rules also apply to computers at school, in the library, and at a friend's house. She should have heard these plenty of times during elementary school.

She should:

- never, ever give out her first and last name, address, grade, age, or the school she attends.
- stay out of chat rooms.
- use instant messaging (IM) only with those names she recognizes; never a stranger even if he claims to be a boy her age from another school.
- tell her parents immediately if she's mistakenly gotten into an

uncomfortable situation; don't try to hide it.
- not write anything on the Internet she wouldn't say directly to the person to whom she is texting.
- not get involved in mean conversations or online bullying. Tell her parents. Bullying can be dangerous.
- not break school rules or the law.
- report any incidence of pornography immediately to her parents. Don't share it or show it to anyone else.

Finally, if it feels wrong, it's wrong.
If it makes her uncomfortable, it's wrong.

She must remember that what she posts on the Internet stays there forever. *Forever.* Be sure she remembers that.

Fifty Common Text Abbreviations (Caution: R-Rated)

- 2moro = Tomorrow
- 2nite = Tonight
- 9 = Parent is watching
- 99 = Parent is no longer watching
- BI5 = Back In five
- BRB = Be Right Back
- BTW = By The Way
- B4N = Bye For Now
- BCNU = Be Seeing You
- BFF = Best Friends Forever
- CT = Can't Talk or Can't Text
- CYA = Cover Your Ass or See Ya
- DBEYR = Don't Believe Everything You Read

- DILLIGAS = Do I Look Like I Give A Sh*t
- F2T = Free to Talk
- FTF = That's Funny or Face To Face
- GR8 = Great
- J/K = Just Kidding
- L8R = Later
- LMAO = Laughing My Ass Off
- MUAH = (sound of a kiss)
- NP = No Problem or Nosy Parents
- RBTL = Read Between The Lines
- OMG = Oh My God
- LOL = Laughing Out Loud
- PLZ = Please
- PRW = Parents aRe Watching
- ROTFLMAO = Rolling On (the) Floor Laughing My Ass Off
- SMH = Shaking My Head
- SITD = Still In The Dark
- SOL = Sh*t Out (of) Luck; Sooner Or Later

- STBY = Sucks To Be You
- sup = what's up
- SWAK = Sealed With A Kiss
- TAW = Teachers Are Watching
- TBT = Throw Back Thursday
- THX = Thanks
- TIR = Teacher In Room
- TMI = Too Much Information
- TTYL = Talk To You Later
- TYVM = Thank You Very Much
- VBG = Very Big Grin
- WEG = Wicked Evil Grin
- WYWH = Wish You Were Here
- WTH = What The Hell
- WTF = What The F**k
- XOXO = Hugs and Kisses
- YB = You Bitch
- YOLO = You Only Live Once
- zerg = to gang up on somebody

Get a complete list of all current text abbreviations at http://www.netlingo.com/acronyms.php

Social Media

Facebook (http://www.Facebook.com)

It seems that just about everyone has a Facebook account. It will be difficult to keep your child from being a part of Facebook. Kids inform each other of their life events through Facebook, arrange meetings, plan parties. Your daughter could be excluded because she can't get on Facebook. It would be wonderful if you can hold off Facebook until your daughter is ready for high school. If you've done that, good for you.

Experts recommend that students not have Facebook accounts until they reach high school. That's a terrific idea but not very practical. She will not want to wait that long especially since "all" of her friends have accounts. If you choose to allow her to have a Facebook account, help her set up her Facebook account, for which she must give you the password and if she changes the password, she must give it to you. Additionally, she must accept you as a friend.

Use her first and maybe her middle name and provide no other private information. Go to settings and make it so that only friends can see or respond to her posts. Ask someone who's familiar with the settings on Facebook to help you, if necessary.

She may not accept a friend request unless she already knows who the person is. Otherwise, she is opening the door to unsavory characters viewing all her information and photographs. If she puts photographs on her Facebook site, she should not tag them (identify each person). If your daughter is tagged in a photograph, it can be removed.

Most parents do not realize that there is a minimum age requirement to join Facebook. Members must be at least 13 years old, according to Facebook's Terms of Service. So how do so many of your daughter's friends become

members? A recent study found that the majority of underage children were supported and assisted by their parents to lie about their age. Of the parents who were interviewed, most didn't know that there was an age minimum and other parents believed that it is up to them to decide at what age their child should become part of an online service or social media.
http://journals.uic.edu/ojs/index.php/fm/article/view/3850/3075

    This is the most popular media site in the world, yet its use among young people is on the decline, probably because they don't want to use the same social network their parents are using.

One of the problems of Facebook is the issue of bullying. This type of behavior is unacceptable on Facebook but it exists and can be very hurtful to the children to whom the comments are directed. Parents should ensure that their own child is not doing any of the bullying and, upon viewing bullying, should report to you. Bullying is dangerous.

Facebook has partnered with suicide prevention and mental health experts.

YouTube (http://www.YouTube.com)

This site allows users to post video. Some are home made videos and others are segments of TV shows, performing singers and comedians, lots of "how to" videos, and some just for little kids.

You may notice in this book that I recommend that your daughter go to YouTube to get hints on how to apply makeup. There are lots of good things about YouTube. But there are unsavory videos that may crop up for your daughter.

You Tube has a Safety Mode that filters out mature or age-restricted video. No plan is foolproof but this program helps identify and hide content. Here's how to turn it on:
https://support.google.com/youtube/answer/174084?hl=en

Twitter (http://www.Twitter.com)

Rising in popularity, Twitter does not have an age requirement and does not ask for age, birthdate, or gender during registration. Founded in 2006, it allows people all around the world to share comments instantly. Most of what is written on Twitter is available to everyone, although settings can be used to change that option. However, most twitter users allow their tweets to be seen by everyone and even retweeted (someone who likes your comment will copy it and repost it).

It is very important that your daughter understand that she really needs to think before she writes and posts a tweet. On Facebook, you can delete your post. On Twitter, your comment is there for anyone to read. It may be a good practice to suggest that your child write out (or type) her comments before submitting them to Twitter. That's not a bad idea for Facebook posts either. She can then copy and paste her comment into a Facebook post or tweet after you review them, until she gets into the habit of doing it herself.

Vine (<http://www.vine.co>**)**

A lot like YouTube and easy to use. But it's even easier for kids to view content they probably shouldn't see. iTunes rates Vine for members 17+. And the reasons, taken directly from the App Store on iTunes:

- Frequent/Intense Sexual Content or Nudity
- Infrequent/Mild Horror/Fear Themes
- Infrequent/Mild Realistic Violence
- Infrequent/Mild Alcohol, Tobacco, or Drug Use or Reference
- Infrequent/Mild Mature/Suggestive Themes
- Infrequent/Mild/ Cartoon or Fantasy Violence
- Infrequent/Mild Simulated Gambling
- Infrequent/Mild Medical/Treatment Information

- Infrequent/Mild Profanity or Crude Humor

How would you like this for your tween daughter? I think not.

Snapchat (http://www.snapchat.com)

Users can send photos and messages that self-destruct. Unfortunately, all this does is facilitate sexting by making it seem risk free. There is a parents' guide on the website at https://www.snapchat.com/static_files/parents.pdf.

http://www.Ask.fm

Recently purchased by Ask.com, the new owners promise to improve the safety on the site. Users can post any questions they choose, and keep their name anonymous. Other users respond to the questions, but the questioner has to decide what answer fits her question.

Kik (http://www.kik.com**)**

This is an instant messaging (IM) program for smart phones. Members can send and receive messages, share photos, sketches, webpages, and other content. Members must register a user name. However, this site has run into the problem of accidentally distributed explicit images and texts. OinkText has been linked to Kik which allows communication with strangers. The texts also display the writer's read name so it's

better to sign up with a fictitious name.
http://en.wikipedia.org/wiki/Kik_Messenger

Secret.ly and Whisper.sh

Similar in that they encourage users to share their innermost feelings, fears, dangers, lies, you name it. Secret is for 13+. Whisper is 17+.

http://www.Fessapp.com

"Only students allowed in, no fesses allowed out". Fess is short for confession or secret. This app is exclusively for high school students. It claims to be anonymous but to verify the user's age, she must do it through facebook. So how is it anonymous? There is much to worry about with this app including bullying, obscene language. It does have a list of rules when you log on of issues it will not permit including violating human rights or copyright laws and pornography that's offensive. One user wrote "It's like crack. Once you start, you can't stop." (from the website ad)

YikYak (www.Yik Yak.com)

Has become very popular on college campuses. No sign-up is required. It boasts "no profile, no password, it's all anonymous." It asks the user to verify that she is at least 17 years old before downloading the app but plenty of younger people are members.

It focuses on users within a 1.5 mile area so that the communications are all local. However, it reveals the user's location. It is known for cyberbullying, and explicit sexual comments. (www.commonsensemedia.org)

As of this writing, Dr. Keith Ablow, psychiatrist, feels this is the most dangerous "app" of all. Comments are totally anonymous. ([fox.com](fox.com)) Anyone can say anything about anyone else and there's nothing that can be done about it because it's anonymous. The person who is being written about has to either ignore the comments or try to defend herself. It is becoming popular in high schools and middle schools and Yik Yak claims it is working to ban students younger than 17 from the use of their social application.

Anyone using Yik Yak can turn a school (college campus, high school, middle school, and who knows – elementary school) into a virtual chat room where everyone in her geographic area can see untruthful, mean comments immediately. According to Dr. Ablow, this has become the ultimate tool for bullies. This would be a good tool to discourage your daughter from using.
(http://www.huffingtonpost.com/news/yik-yak/)

www.textnow.com and www.text.me

If you must take your phone away from your daughter for whatever reason, don't think she can't send and receive text messages. On the computer, she can go to either of these sites (and I'm sure there are others), set up a free account, and have access to send and receive text messages. Be sure if you have decided that she cannot text for a period of time, that she is not using the computer to do it.

Meetme.com

Offers the user the chance to "chat and meet new people." Is this okay with you?

Charm

Advertises "real people, real fast, real fun".

Roar

For girls only aged 17+. It claims to be a "kinder chat".

There are so many more! By the time you read this book or even just this section, more text apps will have been created, some will have fallen by the wayside, and popularity will swing often. If you visit www.wikipedia.org, go to "Comparison of Instant Messaging Clients", not necessarily to read all about them, but just to see how many there are.

Forever

Forbidding something makes it irresistible so explain why something, in this case Internet sites, is a bad idea.

It's almost impossible to be anonymous in a digital world. Threats made on Yik Yak have been traced and students arrested. Being charged with a terrorist threat has a huge effect on college resumes or job applications.

Just as we mentioned with IM (Instant Messaging) and Facebook, your digital footprint is forever. This may be a difficult concept for tweens but if you push it enough, they'll get it.

> *"Is it true? Is it kind? Is it necessary?"*
>
> --Socrates

Lunches

Shopping

She's old enough now to select and pack her own lunch. Go grocery shopping together. Point out that buying individual items is more expensive in the long run than purchasing one large pack. Let her choose some of her favorite items. Follow a budget.

After a few times of grocery shopping with a parent, your daughter may decide she doesn't want to go any more and you "know what I like". Discourage her from staying home. If she insists, and if you give in, purchase what you think makes good, healthy lunches. If she discovers that she doesn't like what you purchased, she'll soon start shopping with you again. And she should bear this responsibility.

Packing

Your daughter should pack her own lunch, getting in the habit of packing her lunch the night before school. If she waits until the morning, she might not have time or may just throw anything in her sack. Regardless of how tired or busy she claims she is, force the issue that she pack her lunch the night before school.

Just because she's packing her own lunch doesn't mean you shouldn't check out the contents. There should be a fruit or vegetable (or both). If she doesn't have any, add it. Remind her to include a napkin or paper towel. Just like in elementary school, under no circumstances should she share or exchange food with anyone, mainly because of allergies.

Lunch Money

She may not always want to pack a lunch, and there may be something offered at school that she likes. But how do you pay for it?

Starting when she completes fifth grade, as soon as fifth grade ends, in other words immediately, place a jar in your cupboard. Every time, and I mean every time, you come home with change in your pocket or purse, drop it into the jar. You'll be surprised at how quickly that jar will fill up.

When your daughter needs lunch money, you'll have a supply to start school and carry you through the first part of the year. If you have precocious children, you may want to put your jar on a high shelf so they don't help themselves! This is strictly lunch money for your daughter and even you shouldn't use it for other reasons.

Following the Menu

If she has selected perishable foods for her lunches, then she must pack her lunches and not let food go to waste because she changed her mind. It will be easier once you get the monthly lunch menu and she clearly marks the days she wants to eat lunch at school. You'll know how much grocery shopping to do. She needs to follow the menu selections, unless she decides to pack a lunch instead of buying. But if she selects more days to buy lunch than originally planned, food will go to waste and your money will disappear sooner.

Losing Weight

If you notice that your daughter is losing weight, ask her if she'd like something different for lunch. When she brings home her lunch sack, check to see if she's eaten her lunch, although you can't be sure because she may have shared her lunch even if she's not supposed to or have thrown the contents away.

Call the school and speak with the guidance counselor. Ask her to check that your daughter is eating her lunches. She can do this easily by visiting the lunchroom and walking around, while keeping an eye on your daughter. If she notices that your daughter is not eating, she may want to meet with her one on one to discuss any concerns your daughter has. How is school going? Is she having any problems with any classes or teachers? What about other students? Would she like a different place to sit for lunch?

Is she eating dinner? Does she snack after school? If she continues to lose weight, she may be suffering from anorexia or another condition. It's important to have your physician conduct a check up and complete some blood work. A urine sample will help to know if she's gotten involved with drugs.

Gaining Weight

On the other hand, if your daughter is noticeably gaining weight, check what she selects for lunch. Then look at what you serve for meals at home. You may be aiding the problem by serving pasta, potatoes, and other foods that could play a part in her gaining weight. Be sure you have healthy choices for breakfast, lunch, and after school snack.

Encourage her, without nagging, to get involved in a physical activity. Put her in charge of taking the dog for a 15-30 minute walk every day. If she continues to gain weight, a doctor's appointment is called for. Do not berate her and especially don't make fun of her or allow her siblings to make unkind comments.

Caloric Intake

Whether too heavy or not weighing enough, the typical middle school girl needs between 1500 and 1800 calories a day. She may need more if she's active or experiencing a growth spurt.

During a typical day, your daughter should eat:

Whole grains
2 ½ cups vegetables
1 ½ cups fruit
3 cups milk
5 ounces meat or beans

Avoid refined grains as in corn flakes, pastas, pretzels, white rice, white bread, and rolls. Substitute wild rice or whole grain rice, wheat corn flakes, barley, and rolled oats. Rolled oats make great cookies. Just search the Internet and you'll find lots of recipes.

Healthy Snacks

Stock up on healthy snacks that are not perishable, such as rice cakes, whole grain cereal, dried fruit, nuts, peanut butter, low fat popcorn and perishables such as fruit, yogurt, cheese, and vegetables, especially carrots, celery, cucumbers, and peppers. I recommend peeling the cucumbers because the skin is often tough. Then you can cut them into thin chips or long strips. You can also use a potato peeler and peel the cucumber lengthwise until you get to the seeds in the middle. Turn the cucumber and peel from the other side. Making vegetables in this style are very popular with kids and can be added to a sandwich. You can do the same with carrots. Use your peeler and peel down the length of a carrot over and over. It creates very thin strips that are fun to eat and great for sandwiches.

Carrots, celery, and peppers can be cut into thin strips in advance and placed in the refrigerator. Celery can be fun by filling it with peanut butter or cashew butter. Sometimes add raisins onto the peanut butter. This treat is called bugs on a log.

Dried fruit instead of potato chips is a good substitute.

Substitutions for Peanut Butter

Some schools have become "peanut free" schools, not allowing peanut butter or anything that includes peanuts due to the high incidence of allergic reactions to peanuts. If your school is one, you might want to substitute cashew butter, soy butter, or cookie butter instead of peanut butter.

Leftovers

Don't forget about leftovers from dinner. Your daughter might enjoy the break from the usual lunch with a salad, pasta salad (take leftover pasta, add some olive oil and vegetables), include leftover cheese and meat in a salad or make an antipasto by adding some peppers, olives, and a sprinkle of olive oil.

Sandwiches

Try different ways to make sandwiches by not using white bread. Use whole wheat or 12-grain bread, pancakes, quesadillas, tortillas, or even crackers. Use cookie cutters and cut out different shapes for the sandwiches. Yes, even your growing up daughter will enjoy that.

Calcium

Offer calcium rich food. Most tweens only get 50% of what is recommended. Offer milk, yogurt, and cheese. (tweenparenting.about.com)

Drinks

For lunch drinks, choose water or unsweetened iced tea, not soda or sugar-filled fruit juices. Use an ice pack to keep everything cold, but it will sweat so if your daughter's using a brown paper bag, you may want to wrap the ice pack in something that will keep it from getting the bag wet and ripping it. You might try a zip loc bag or saran wrap. You can also open the water bottle and pour half of the water into another container. Place the water bottle in the freezer overnight, and then add the extra water in the morning before she leaves for school. It will keep the water cold but it also may sweat so wrap it too. You don't have to wrap items that sweat if your daughter uses a reusable lunch sack and packs each item separately.

Fruit

Include grapes, berries, apples, oranges, and bananas with dipping sauce. Low fat ranch dressing or plain or vanilla yogurt are great options for the dip. There are perfect-sized containers for dip that are available in any grocery store: they're clear with a blue lid and are made to hold baby food.

Don't Throw That Away!

Remind your daughter to bring home ice packs or any reusable containers!

Speaking of bringing things home or not throwing something away, if your daughter wears a retainer and removes it while she eats, she must be extra careful where she places her retainer. Placing it on a napkin is not a good idea. After a vivid lunchtime conversation, your daughter will gather together all of the paper from her lunch and throw it away. That includes the retainer. If she has a lunch sack, have her put the retainer into her lunch sack or her handbag. At the very least, she can put it into her pocket.

My Story

When I was a principal, a sixth grade girl came to me in tears at the end of the lunch period.

"I accidentally threw away my retainer," she wailed. "My mother's going to kill me."

I sent her off to class, obtained plastic gloves from the custodian, and began rummaging through each and every gigantic, silver garbage can filled with leftovers of all kinds along with paper. Of course, it was spaghetti day. The adults told me I was crazy, just to let it go, but I didn't want her mother to kill her! By the time I got to the third garbage can, I had created a method for going through all the napkins in search of her retainer. I found it, cleaned it, and took it to the student. She was forever – or at that moment -- grateful and did not lose her retainer for the rest of the school year!

Who Do I Sit With At Lunch?

This is a common concern of most girls during the first few days of school. One suggestion is to be friendly during class changes and then find a table with one or more of the girls who were friendly back to her. I think this is problematic. Other girls may have said hello but may not want her to sit with them or have saved the seats for others. Being turned away from a table can be very embarrassing for your daughter.

Once she knows what her schedule is and what period she has lunch, I suggest she make a lunch date. Before the start of school, have her seek out other girls she already knows from elementary school or activities and find ones with the same lunch time. Then make a date to save a seat for each other. This will allay her fears of being turned down or eating alone. It won't take long before she meets other girls and widens her circle of lunch dates.

Make Dried Fruit

If you don't have a dehydrator, you can still make your own dried fruit. When you read the long list of ingredients in dried fruit sold in grocery stores, you'll want to make your own.

Select fruit that is ripe but not overripe. Peel apples, peaches, and pears. I peel peaches only.

Remove the seeds and cut away any damaged areas. For an apple, you can use a corer to take out the center, and then cut the apple into full size rings. For other pieces of fruit, try to cut them all thinly and of similar width.

Place parchment paper over cookie sheets and place your fruit on them, being sure the pieces don't touch.

Set your oven between 150-200 degrees. Some recipes call for the oven door to be left open, but I keep it closed.

Don't get impatient and turn up the heat. You don't want cooked fruit!

Every hour (or more often if you prefer) move the cookie sheets to different shelves. Set your kitchen timer so you don't forget. Some preparers flip the fruit part way through the process. I do not.

For fruit that turns brown, soak it whole for about ten minutes in a solution of the juice of one lemon and twelve cups of water. If you have not peeled the fruit (like apples), you'll need to cut them before placing them in the lemon water.

Wait for the fruit to dry. You don't want it to be hard; you want it chewy. It may take all day (6-8 hours) but except for moving the cookie sheets you can go about your daily routine.

When you remove the fruit from the oven, let it out on the counter for about an hour until cooled.

Berries can be dried whole, except for strawberries.

You can get more information from the Internet.

"Middle school was probably my hardest time. I was trying to fit in for so long until high school when I realized that trying to fit into this one image of perfection was never going to make me happy."

--Maiara Walsh

Make up

When your daughter enters middle school, she'll want to wear makeup, if she hasn't asked already. Wanting to wear makeup is a "coming of age" event. If you say no, chances are she'll do it anyway. She'll buy some cheap, inappropriate cosmetics and apply them poorly on the bus or in the bathroom at school. Can you just imagine the results?

Where to Begin

Wearing

You and she might fare better if you buy her a few items, such as a light pink lip gloss and eyeshadow that's a peachy or pink color. Then show her the proper way to apply this makeup. Don't take for granted that she will just know. Have fun doing it. However, if she does say to you "I know how to do it", then step back and later suggest that she might enjoy watching some YouTube videos on makeup application.

If she asks for mascara or eyeliner, tell her one step at a time. You can eventually add brown mascara. Although more difficult to remove, I recommend waterproof mascara so it doesn't migrate over her cheeks during the day. Teach her how to use this makeup too. Only one coat of mascara and the mascara doesn't go with her to school.

Cleansing

Purchase a gentle eye makeup remover and teach her how to use it. I would discourage any other makeup for as long as you can hold out! When she and you are ready, add a light pink or peach blush. You can try to control the use of makeup and you may be successful – or not. You may want to avoid a moisturizer because many of them add oil to the skin, and moisturizer could make an acne problem worse.

My Story

I forbade my younger daughter from plucking her eyebrows.

"Your eyebrows are just fine."

"But the other girls pluck theirs."

"That's because their eyebrows aren't as nice as yours."

"Mine are thick and look like a kid's."

"Well, you still are a kid and you're not ready for this."

"I think you're the one who's not ready."

And off she stomped. I thought that was the end of it. Boy, was I naïve then.

A few mornings later she walked downstairs and there she was – without eyebrows. She had plucked her eyebrows until each one probably had two hairs each. She had completely removed them. And, of course, I reacted poorly again.

"What is the matter with you? I told you not to pluck your eyebrows."

"Well, it's too late now."

"It's too late, young lady, because you didn't listen to me. Do you see how you look? Have you looked into a mirror?"

"You mean because I didn't obey you. You're not right about everything, you know."

"Well, obviously, I was right about this because you look terrible. What is the matter with you?"

And away she stomped again, this time crying.

After I came to my senses, I went to her room to talk about it.

"What do you want?" she mumbled.

"I know what I told you and what I just said. That doesn't solve our immediate problem."

"I don't have a problem."

"Well, let's just say you'd like to have some eyebrows for school on Monday."

"I can't do that and I look hideous, according to you."

"Well, then, let's fix it."

"How?"

"Let's go shopping. We'll find an eyebrow pencil that's close to your real color and then I'll teach you how to put it on."

"Really?"

"Yes, really, And when your brows grow back, how about letting me help you pluck them?"

"Um … maybe."

That was good enough for the moment. We went shopping and purchased an eyebrow pencil and sharpener, then returned to her room and went to work. I let her do one eyebrow on her own and I did the other eyebrow. She couldn't help but notice the difference. She washed her face and I explained to her how to tell how long a brow should be and how you measure it depending upon your eye. It took her a few times but she got the hang of it and was very proud of herself. I finished the lesson by reminding her to wash her face every night and that when she plucks, to do it after a shower.

I heard her on the phone telling her girlfriend the proper method for using an eyebrow pencil.

Her brows did grow back and she allowed me to pluck the stray ones, but she continued to wear her eyebrow pencil.

How could I have avoided all of this? When she asked to pluck her brows, I should have sat with her and combed her eyebrows. Then, while she watched in the mirror, I could have plucked the stray hairs. That might very well have been the end of it. Maybe she would have done it anyway. Maybe not. But I could have avoided harsh words and hurt feelings.

I allowed her to take her lip gloss and blush to school, but nothing else. I'm no fool: she may have gotten them past me a few times.

Since she's started to wear makeup, remind her not to share her makeup with anyone else and not to let anyone use her makeup, for health reasons.

Shaving

This is the time she may ask to shave her legs. If she does, agree but teach her how to do it. Use single edged razors instead of double-edged to lower the chance of nicking herself (don't forget to shave tops of toes too!). If she uses disposable razors, remind her that 4-5 times is enough before they should be disposed of properly. She also doesn't need to shave her legs every day. Teach her to shave under her arms. Give her shaving cream instead of having her use soap. She should avoid moisturizer immediately after shaving her legs.

> "Eighty percent of skin damage occurs before the age of eighteen."
>
> --http://www.thegrommet.com

Acne

Remind your daughter to wash her face every night, every morning, and after every sporting event or practice, especially if she's started to wear makeup.

Just as important, she needs to keep her hands clean and refrain from touching her face with her hands. If she does get acne, very typical at this age, impress upon her the damage she can do to her skin by picking at or popping pimples. Explain what a pock mark looks like and that it's permanent.

If her acne really bothers her, purchase some gentle, over the counter cleanser that is oil free and labeled "noncomedogenic" which will not clog her pores and cause more issues. One of the most popular and reasonably priced is over the counter "Neutrogena's Oil Free Acne Wash" that's left on the skin for a minute or two to penetrate the skin before it's rinsed off.

You might look for a gentle cleanser that has the ingredient of salicylic acid or benzoyl peroxide. However, these ingredients may cause a skin reaction so it should be tried on a patch of skin over 24 hours before using it as directed. Other brands include Cetaphyl Gentle Skin Cleanser and Dove Sensitive Cleansing Cloths (great for her backpack when she has sports practice after school).

Tell her never to use body lotion on her face. It's too harsh. Nor should she borrow your moisturizer or cleanser; they're especially formulated for a woman your age and not a tween. If she insists on a moisturizer, turn to the Cetaphyl brand again for a gentle facial moisturizer. If you have the money to spend, an expensive but good brand of moisturizer is Willa, Face the Day. It's oil free, PABA free, chemical free, and fragrance free.

Any moisturizer should contain sunscreen. She should cleanse gently and not scrub her face as that could damage her skin. If she uses it every morning, every night, and after sports, following directions, and there's no improvement after about six weeks, then it might be time to visit the family doctor or a dermatologist.

Be sympathetic. Statements not to make include "This too shall pass", "It doesn't look that bad", and "You can hardly notice it." She won't believe you and will be offended by your remarks. Try something like "I'm sorry you have to go through this" or "How can I help?" You might even tell her a story of yours from when you were a middle school student and how your complexion cleared. Show her photos of you in middle school and then at the end of high school.

Remember to tell her that she's beautiful and compliment her often and specifically. Instead of "You look nice", try "I like the combination of that skirt and top. It looks great." Be specific. There's more of a chance that she'll believe you.

> *"Once your kid reaches middle school, parents are really supposed to fade out of the social picture."* Claire Scovell LaZebnik

Parents' Roles

As tweens push away from their parents and are pulled towards their peers, they still need the support and the love of their parents, although they may not act that way. Up until now, you have been in the driver's seat and your daughter has held the passenger seat, going where you want to go, when you want to go. Sometimes she got to read the map, but even then, you might have changed your mind. You control the car and you do the driving.

In middle school, you are often unceremoniously pushed out of the driver's seat. Now she is in charge. She has control of the car. If you're lucky, you'll get to sit in the passenger seat. But more likely, her best friend (BFF) will have that seat and you'll be relegated to the back seat. Just remember that when she looks in the rearview mirror, she'll feel more in control if she sees you there.

Be prepared, when she is in the mood, to listen to her. Being a good listener is one of your most important jobs during this period of her life.

Tweens and Toddlers

Tweens are a lot like toddlers. They might throw a tantrum or act like they're going through the terrible two's one minute and be very sweet the next. They need you to suggest healthy snacks for them to eat, and also tell them when it's time to go to bed. They will fight you over these decisions, just as they did when they were toddlers. You'll grow tired of hearing "No" and "That's not fair!"

Tweens will go through a growth spurt, just like toddlers. They're going to expend a lot of energy and need more food and snacks then ever before. You'll notice. And in expending this energy, they will suffer from exhaustion but never admit it. When tweens are hungry or exhausted, they get crabby, just like a toddler.

To help your child, and cut down on the number of tantrums or crabby moods, provide good healthy food for breakfast, lunch, snacks, and supper. Kids will reach for healthy snacks if you don't have food high in fat and salt. Bring those kinds of snacks home and the healthy snacks are forgotten.

Dinner

I still believe that families should eat dinner together. It's that one chance during a hectic day to actually see each other, talk, and listen. My children and I always sat down for dinner during the week but it'd be a less formal gathering on the weekends. No one was permitted to answer the phone. I answered and took messages. The kids couldn't call back until everyone completed dinner and the table cleared. This was before cell phones. Now I would make them turn off their cell phones for dinner.

Sleep

Another way to help your child is to ensure that she gets enough sleep. Tweens need about nine hours of sleep a night, and might need even more during growth spurts. You'll know that she's not getting enough sleep if it takes her longer to do her homework, she is argumentative, and you have trouble making her pay attention to what you say. Tweens, just like toddlers, will complain that they don't want to go to bed. As Nancy Darling wrote on Psychologytoday.com, "I didn't say you were tired, I said it was bedtime."

Remember to remove distractions from the bedroom. The cell phone is brought downstairs and charged, the laptop is brought downstairs, no video or handheld games are played in bed. Bed is for sleeping. Using any of these electronics will stimulate your tween's brain and make it more difficult for her to sleep. Reading a book is a good way to transition to bed.

> *"School prepares you for the real world...*
> *which also bites."*
> — Jim Benton

Parent/Teacher Conferences

As you know, your child has more than one teacher. If you don't know who to schedule a conference with, select the homeroom teacher and ask him to invite any other teachers who might add to the conversation. If the school doesn't schedule parent conferences, you should do so by the end of the first marking period. Decide ahead of time the questions you want answered or the concerns you have. Some might include:

- Do you group children by ability?
- If so, what group is my child in?
- Does she stay with the same group all day?
- How is what she's taught different from the top group (if she's not already in the top group)?
- Is she working to her ability?
- Does she miss class? Is she often late?
- Does she submit homework on time and done correctly?
- Does she get along with her classmates?

- Does she pay attention during class?
- Does she come prepared for class, with all her materials (book, notebook, pen or pencil, etc.)
- What can I do at home to help her to be successful?

Give the teacher(s) your email address and ask for theirs. Request email updates.

" ... There were times when, in middle school, I didn't have a lot of friends. But my mom was always my friend. Always."
--Taylor Swift

Prepare Your Child for Middle School

Your daughter, whether or not she admits it, has trepidation about leaving her well-known elementary school and entering middle school. Talk with her about all the good parts of a middle school: there'll be clubs and organizations for her to join, as well as extracurricular activities such as basketball, track, and cheerleading. She'll experience different teaching styles and learn many new things. She'll meet students her age or near her age and become friends with many while she learns to understand others.

New Friends

Remind her that she's growing up and belongs in the middle school. She'll learn to be independent. She'll make new friends while keeping her old friends. She'll be old enough to stay home alone and to babysit to make her own money.

Start the new or revised hours for going to bed and getting up at least a week before school starts. When they get up early, they can really take their time preparing for the day and can even nap in the afternoon. Help them to get used to going to bed earlier than they probably have all summer.

Role Play

What will she do if:

- she can't get her locker open and she's going to be late for class: get to class on time and admit she can't open her locker to get out her homework assignment. Usually, a teacher will send her back out to

her locker with a classmate who will help her open her locker.
- she left her homework at home: face the consequences at school.
- some of the popular girls are making fun of her: walk away. Talk to her parents about how she's feeling. Don't let them see you get upset.
- she's invited to an after school party without parents: practice with her what her response is. "I'd love to go but I'm not allowed". "I'd go but I have too much homework" or the plain truth "My parents won't allow me to go to a party when there's no adult".
- she's being bullied: practice with her what she can say in return to

someone bullying her "Your opinion doesn't matter to me" or "I'm fine, thank you"; she can also try ignoring the person doing the bullying but that may or may not work. Make her positive comment and walk away.

- she's being encouraged to bully another student: practice with her what she can say, such as "I don't want to bully anyone", "I don't think it's right" and walk away. If she stays there while the bullying is going on, she might be part of the problem. Plus, it would be good for her to report the bullying if it happens in school. She may get bullied for reporting it, but she

needs to know that she's doing the right thing.
- she doesn't understand the homework assignment: if time allows after class, approach the teacher and ask if you can meet with him because she is confused by the assignment or when she gets home, she can call a friend to help her understand. Parents can be helpful too but she shouldn't always count on her parents to solve her problems.
- she doesn't understand the lesson that just took place: same as above.
- she forgot her lunch and has no money: ask if she may get lunch and pay for it the next day. One way to avoid this is to give her lunch

money for one day, put it in an envelope or small coin purse and have her put it in her locker or backpack. She shouldn't use it unless she has forgotten her lunch money; she should not depend on it but rather forget she has it. Once she uses it, she brings it home and gets money back in the purse.

- she tries out to be a cheerleader and doesn't make it but her best friend does: although she won't agree, she tried and that's what matters. Practice having her compliment her friend who made the squad. She can think about another activity, maybe the band or band front or majorette, that she might enjoy.

Create Her "Materials for School" Box

Just as you may have done when she was in elementary school, she's going to need items for school.

- Pencils with erasers, sharpened, and a pencil sharpener; number two pencils really are the best for every day use
- Pens, inexpensive ones
- Highlighters, at least two different colors
- Colored pencils, sharpened
- Ruler (six inch will fit into almost any pouch)

- Hole punch (small plastic one that will only punch a page or two at a time; it'll fit in her backpack)
- Scissors
- Scotch tape
- Index cards
- Post-it notes
- School journal or assignment book (that includes a calendar)

Put everything in a shoebox with a lid and place it in a convenient location. Remind her to tell you when she runs out of anything.

Wait to purchase notebooks and other items until she starts school and finds out the requirements of each teacher. It will make your and her life easier if she has the basics when she needs them.

She may choose to color code her subjects and have a different colored notebook cover for each class and match the color with a highlighter and a colored pen, if you can spring for that.

"... The whole cheerleader, football player, clique-y thing ... was terrifying. Those people were so scary. They're the scariest kinds of people because they are idolized by their peers."

--Zoe Kravitz

Social Life

"Think fifth grade was a bumpy ride? Welcome to middle school, the roller coaster of puberty, peer pressure, and social insecurity." This statement was written by Rose Garrett from her article "Your Middle Schooler's Social Life".

Have you ever played "Whisper Down the Lane"? A group of people or children stand next to each other in a straight line. The first child is given a piece of paper with a sentence written on it. She must whisper that sentence to the child next to her, who must whisper it to the child next to him, who must whisper it … you get the idea. The last child announces what the sentence is and the first child announces what the sentence should be. It can be a funny experiment.

It's not quite as funny in middle school. If you are searching for the definition of the word gossip, listen to middle school girls. They "know" everything about everyone important or who matters and every one of them believes what is told to them by each other. They believe as truth what their classmates tell them about dating, sex, and yes, even school.

Life in middle school is filled with drama; it's like a tween soap opera. Why? Tweens tend to feel very insecure but may not be able to identify that feeling. Each girl wants to be praised, wants to have lots of friends, and wants to be the center of attention – everywhere. They want to feel a sense of reassurance that they are okay, they are normal.

Girls can be very catty one day and friends with another girl the next day. Whereas boys bully pretty much publicly, girls are much more clever. What they do and say about other girls is tough to pick up, unless one of the girls tells you. That's not probable because she doesn't want to be the next one on the bad list or stay on that list. So girls take the name-calling, ignoring, and rude behavior and try to ignore it or just accept it. How sad. The girl who makes the most fun of others is also the one who is most insecure. She needs to pull down the girls around her so she looks better and is the center of attention.

"Kids can be so nasty to each other …
especially girls. Whatever happened to girls building one another up instead of tearing each other down? As a mom, it makes me furious."

--Gina Hoppes, Parent of Middle School Girl

Stress

Alphabetically, this topic falls near the end of this book, but it is one of the most important topics.

Tweens feel an enormous amount of stress: stress to get good grades, stress to have friends, stress about liking a boy, stress about losing friends, stress about living through middle school, stress about being late for class, stress about forgetting something, stress about doing well in extracurricular activities, stress about making the team, stress about ... You get the idea.

Tween girls, more than boys, tend to be stressed about almost everything in their lives. For most girls, you won't have to tell her that you expect good grades; she expects that more than you do.

But the overwhelming feeling among girls is their desire to have friends, to belong to a group. No longer are their parents or family the focus of their happiness. Now it's all about who is and who is not her friend.

Self-esteem is a tenuous concept in middle school. Girls gain their self-esteem from other girls. They no longer get it from their families, their church, their activities, and their successes. It all revolves around friends. And that means that their self-esteem is tied, unfortunately, to cliques. Internally, they study where they fall on the popularity scale. Teasing is one of the worst experiences she can have. Her self-esteem can vary day by day as she "lives with" teasing, cliques, best friends who have new best friends, and maybe even bullying. All of that makes it tough to keep her self-esteem under control, to keep it high.

She looks at herself in the mirror and sees only the imperfections. "If only I were as thin as Mary, I'd be more popular", "If only my breasts were larger, I'd be more popular", "If only my breasts were smaller, I'd be more popular", "If I could just lose some weight, I'd be more popular", "If only mom would let me wear more makeup, I'd be more popular", "If I had cool clothes like Chloe, I'd be more popular", "If only I had extra spending money like Anna has, I'd be more popular". Her thoughts are enough to make anyone act erratically and no wonder she does.

That's why clothes and makeup and the kind of backpack she has are all so very important to her. It's not that she particularly likes the items; she just wants to fit in. She just wants to belong.

Young ladies who lack self-esteem are usually the ones "in charge" of a clique, the leaders. They are the ones who make fun of other girls and tease them, maybe even start rumors about other girls. This all relates to the girl's lack of self-esteem. She builds herself up the only way she knows how: by tearing down everyone around her.

Boys tend to buy into this behavior of the girl in charge. They will continue the teasing, call other girls names to their faces (while girls tend to do it behind their backs), and generally act inappropriately and cruel.

I spoke with a high school girl who told me that the worst thing that happened to her in middle school was a boy coming up to her and saying, "You look like a boy."

He and his friends laughed, pointed, and walked away. She couldn't get his words out of her head. She started research on the Internet on how to enlarge her breasts or at least make herself look like she had breasts. She said that it took a long time before she could look in the mirror and not hate herself.

How do you, as parents, deal with such behavior towards the daughter you love?

First of all, don't overreact. You won't help the situation if you call and complain to the girl's parents or to the school. Although it's possible that they will try to help, their help will only hurt. When the "popular" girls discover that your daughter's mother has complained and involved herself in middle school antics, they will hold your behavior against your daughter. Any chance that they might include her are temporarily crushed. They'll view her as a tattletale, as a girl who can't handle being in middle school, as a big baby. The backlash towards your daughter will be worse than the initial behavior.

So what do you do? You have to stay on the sidelines. Support your daughter. Tell her that she is pretty, that she is talented, that she is so much more than any of these girls realize. Let her know that you are always there for her, no matter what, that you will always listen. Then when she wants to talk, stay true to your word and listen. Don't get distracted with your own cell phone or the other kids. Give her your full attention.

Don't badmouth any of the mean girls. Your daughter will defend them! Remember, they must be doing something right, since they are so popular (that's what your daughter thinks). Keep your focus on her. If she's in the mood, tell her about some of your own experiences and how you overcame your own difficulties but don't downplay hers.

My Story

When I was in high school, I was far from part of the popular cliques, although I had a group of friends. I always admired one girl, Mary. She had everything I lacked: good looks, breasts, lots of guys interested in her, good grades, popular, cheerleader, and member of student council. Her parents were both professionals and well known. I learned when I went to college that I had so much more to offer than I realized when I was in high school. I was successful in my professional life and created a loving personal life. Mary lives and works in the town we grew up in, after getting pregnant near the end of our senior year. She married that summer. She never went to college, never used her abilities that I admired so much. When I think of her, I don't gloat. I feel sorry for her, but maybe her life turned out just the way she wanted. If one to go back and ask the teachers of the day, they all would have chosen Mary, hands down, as the up-and-coming leader in whatever she chose to do.

Middle schoolers can't and shouldn't bear the brunt of not being the most popular kid in school, or even the teacher's pet. They have a lot of living to do and so much changes in that time.

"When faced with senseless drama, spiteful criticisms, and misguided opinions, walking away is the best way to stand up for yourself. To respond with anger is an endorsement of their attitude."

--Dodinsky

Tattoos

If your daughter insists on getting a tattoo, of course you can say no. Will she obey you? Only you can know that. Impress upon her that a tattoo is forever and that if the artist is not tremendously clean and uses an unsterilized needle, it is possible to get hepatitis B or C. There is no cure for hepatitis but medicines can treat it. You might consider hepatitis A and B vaccines to prevent the disease and the concern.

If she's determined to get a tattoo, and the tattoo she wants is in an inconspicuous location and of a small size, consider going with her. That is the only way you can ensure that she goes to a qualified tattoo artist who uses all sterilized equipment.

> *"I know that I am intelligent, because I know that*
> *I know nothing."*
>
> –Socrates

Conclusion

Raising a tween daughter is never easy. I remember my friend and I lamenting the actions of our daughters, claiming "If only we could lock them in the basement until they turned seventeen!" There are wonderful parts to being the parent of a tween. But there are also tough times that you'll both have to muddle through. You may even hear an occasional "I hate you!" that is not true but comes out of frustration of growing up but not quite.

Hopefully, this handbook will help you to think about upcoming events, activities, and questions that you may have to deal with. Use your common sense and sprinkle it with the love you have for her. Remember that if either of you lose your temper, it's up to you, the adult, to end the conversation immediately and continue it at a later time. Losing your temper will lead you to say things you don't mean, make unkind remarks or name calling, or make the situation worse.

When your daughter breaks a house rule (or school rule), handle it as calmly as you can, while doling out the consequence she already knows is coming.

In other words, although your daughter is beginning to feel independent of you and all grown up, you are still driving the car behind the scenes. She just may not realize it.

"In school we learn that mistakes are bad, and we are punished for making them. Yet, if you look at the way humans are designed to learn, we learn by making mistakes. We learn to walk by falling down. If we never fell down, we would never walk."

☐ Robert T. Kiyosaki, *Rich Dad, Poor Dad*

True/False Quiz Answers

1. ____ When there's a problem, it's important to tell your child "We need to talk."
   FALSE. Don't you hate when someone says that to you? You immediately have a flashback over your recent life and wonder what you've done wrong or why you're in trouble. Instead, offer options: "When you have a few minutes, take a break and visit with me" or "Will you set the table tonight?" (great time to talk). "I'm going to the

grocery store (or wherever). Want to come along?"

2. ____ Middle school is just like high school, only the students are younger.
   FALSE. Middle school, if organized and run properly, is not just like a high school. Teachers with elementary degrees as well as secondary degrees can teach in middle schools. There's more attention to the needs and the personal as well as academic growth of the students.

3. ____If a friend hurts your daughter's feelings, the best thing

you can say is "Does it hurt your feelings?"

FALSE. You already know her feelings are hurt, you don't have to ask her again. How about "I'm so sorry you have to go through this" or "Let me know how I can help."

4. ____Allow your daughter to show when she's angry.

   TRUE. If you punish your daughter for displaying anger, she'll learn to hold her feelings inside which is not a good thing. However, that doesn't mean she can go off on a rant about you or the family but she can be frustrated and annoyed.

5. ____If your daughter says she hates her hair, offer, "Why don't you get your hair cut?"
FALSE. By asking that question, you are implying that there is something wrong with her hair. Instead, ask, "What would you like to do?" and "How can I help?" and especially "I think you're beautiful."

6. ____It's time to think about college when your daughter starts middle school.
TRUE. When your child enters middle school, you should be looking ahead to her high school courses that will affect her admission into the college of her choice. If the middle school groups

by ability, try to get your daughter in the advanced math class so she can move into Algebra and Geometry.

7. ____Negotiate with your daughter. TRUE. Sometimes it's okay to negotiate. She may want to stay out past her curfew because of a basketball game she wants to attend. You might negotiate a later curfew with her for just that night but she still has a curfew, just later. Don't, however, negotiate family rules that don't change. She needs to know that some of the house rules are not negotiable.

8.____Do not allow your daughter to go straight to her room after school; this is a sign of rudeness.

FALSE. Your daughter may have had a tough day at school (yes, really) and may need some quiet time, down time, private time. Maybe she has something she wants to discuss with you but wants to get her thoughts together first. Maybe she wants to touch base with her best friend who was absent that day. However, she should say hello when she gets home and should work her way back downstairs after a few minutes to herself.

9.____Your daughter doesn't need to shave in middle school.

FALSE. It's like a rite of passage, along with wearing make up. She will want to shave when she sees that her classmates are already doing it. There's no issue with that. Just be sure you teach her.

10.____Your daughter is old enough to be left home alone.

TRUE. Most tweens can be left home alone for short periods of time (an hour or so). Review the house rules with her first. Check in while you're out. Eventually, you can increase her time home alone. And she will probably start babysitting soon. One thing she should not do is let other people (including her friends) know that she is home alone.

11.____Help your daughter complete her homework.

FALSE. Help your daughter organize her assignments using your and her weekly calendar. Let her do her homework. Allow her to phone a friend if she gets stuck. Review that her work is complete, but it's not like elementary school any more. You don't need to sit with her and work on the homework together.

12.____Don't encourage extracurricular activities; she'll be busy enough   with homework.
FALSE. It's good for your daughter to be involved in a social activity she enjoys. A break from the middle school

academic work is good for her, whether it's basketball, cheerleading, art class, music lessons. Just be careful! Don't allow her to overfill her schedule. That will lead to stress and frustration trying to keep up with everything.

13.____Shop for groceries and pack your daughter's lunch.
FALSE. You and your daughter should shop together for groceries for her lunch. She's old enough to pack her own lunch, although it won't hurt for you to take a peek once in a while.

14.____Anyone can get a Facebook account.

FALSE. Children must be at least 13 years of age to join Facebook.

15.____ The most popular method for communicating between tweens is by phone calls.
FALSE. It may seem like she's on the phone all the time, but the most popular method is texting.

How did you do the first time you took the quiz and the second time? Did your daughter know the answers? Did the questions encourage both of you to discuss the answers?

> *"Nothing could be as hard as middle school."*
> --Zooey Deschanel

Word of Wisdom

Dear World for a Tween

Dear World,

I give to you today a young lady, no longer a child. Do you remember her? She was the little girl with the bright blue dress and big blue eyes and pigtails. She still has those sparkling blue eyes, more curious than ever but tinged with reality.

Please take care of her. She's slipping out of the house today as a brand new teenager. She'll walk down the street to meet her friends. They'll go to school together. I'll stand on the porch and wave but she won't turn around.

She's going to learn about the world and the people who inhabit it. She's going to discover algebra and geometry. She's going to find out what extra activities she likes. She's going to begin to think seriously about her future.

She will learn that her best friend will not always be her best friend. She will learn that teens can be rude and unkind. She'll learn that girls can be mean. She'll learn not to cry.

Now she'll worry about who likes who, what clothes are in, and the popular colors of makeup and nail polish. Up until now, she has looked to me as the center of her world, there to give advice, to guide her, to correct her, to lead her. Now she will look to her friends to be there for her. She no longer will think she needs me.

Today, when the school bell rings, she will walk in as a teenager. She'll learn what it means to belong to a group and what it means to be shunned by that same group. She'll learn that not everyone who smiles at her wants to be her friend and that, a lot of the time, she'll be on her own.

Teach her that it is more honorable to fail than to cheat. Teach her to go her own way, even if everyone else turns away. Teach her to be kind but also to be strong. Teach her to listen to others but make her own decisions. Teach her that she alone is responsible for the decisions she makes. Teach her to believe in herself.

Teach her to laugh. Teach her there's no shame in tears. Teach her to be patient. Help her grow to be wise.

So world, I give you a brand new teenager, once a little girl with shining blue eyes and pigtails. Do you remember her? Help her to keep smiling and discovering the good in this world. Please take care of her.

--Kathleen Molnar Benyo

Resources

This list of book does not include all the wonderful tween books available to you and your daughter. Before purchasing a book for her, read the book jacket and maybe look it up on the Internet. Some of these books are age-appropriate for all tweens, while others work better with daughters aged 13-14, the older side of tween. It is up to you and your daughter to decide what books are appropriate for her.

Fiction List of My Favorite Books for Tweens

Abrahams, Peter. Down the Rabbit Hole (An Echo Falls Mystery).

Aiken, Joan. The Wolves of Willoughby Chase (Wolves Chronicles).
Alexander, Jill S. The Sweetheart of Prosper County.
Bauer, Joan. Squashed.
Bacigalupi, Ship Breaker.
Broach, Elise. Shakespeare's Secret.
Burnett, Frances Hodgson. The Secret Garden.
Collins, Suzanne. The Hunger Games (The Hunger Games, #1).
Connor, Leslie. Waiting for Normal.
Danforth, Emily M. The Miseducation of Cameron Post.
DeVillers, Julia. How My Private Personal Journal Became a Bestseller.
DiCamillo, Kate. Because of Winn Dixie.
Dionne, Erin. Models Don't Eat Chocolate Cookies.

Erskine, Kathryn. Mockingbird.
George, Jean Craighead. Julie of the Wolves.
Green, John. The Fault in Our Stars.
Hale, Shannon. Princess Academy Palace of Stone.
Jahn, Amalie. The Clay Lion (The Clay Lion, #1).
Kadohata, Cynthia. The Thing About Luck.
Kadohata, Cynthia. Weedflower.
Kerr, Philip. The Akhenaten Adventure (Children of the Lamp, #1).
Kittscher, Kristen. The Wig in the Window.
Lee, Harper. To Kill A Mockingbird.
L'Engle, Madeleine. A Wrinkle in Time.
Levine, Gail Carson. Ella Enchanted.
Lowry, Lois. Number the Stars.
Meloy, Maile. The Apothecary.

Miller, Kirsten. <u>Kiki Strike: Inside the Shadow City</u>.
Nielsen, Jennifer A. <u>The False Prince</u> (<u>The Ascendance Trilogy, #1</u>).
Nielsen, Jennifer A. <u>The Runaway King</u> (<u>The Ascendance Trilogy, #2</u>)
O'Dell, Scott. <u>Island of the Blue Dolphins</u>.
Pauley, Kimberly. <u>Sucks to Be Me: The All-True Confessions of Mina Hamilton, Teen Vampire (maybe)</u>.
Paulsen, Gary. <u>Hatchet</u>.
Paulsen, Gary. <u>Notes from the Dog</u>.
Rees, Douglas. <u>Vampire High</u>.
Rowling, J.K. <u>Harry Potter and the Sorcerer's Stone</u> (<u>Harry Potter, #1</u>).
Ryan, Pam Munoz. <u>The Dreamer</u>.
Rowell, Rainbow. <u>Eleanor and Park</u>.
Schrefer, Eliot. <u>Endangered</u>.

Speare, Elizabeth George. The Witch of Blackbird Pond.
Spinelli, Jerry. Maniac Magee.
Stead, Rebecca. When You Reach Me.
Taylor, Mildred D. Roll of Thunder, Hear My Cry.
Turnage, Sheila. Three Times Lucky.
Urban, Linda. A Crooked Kind of Perfect.
Vanderpool, Clare. Moon Over Manifest.
Wein, Elizabeth. Code Name Verity.
Williams-Garcia, Rita. One Crazy Summer.
Woolston, Blythe. The Freak Observer.
Zusak, Markus. The Book Thief.

Great Nonfiction Books for Tweens

Blumberg, Rhoda. Shipwrecked!
Burgan, Michael. Breaker Boys: How a Photograph Helped End Child Labor.

Burns, Loree Griffin. *Tracking Trash: Flotsam, Jetsam, and the Science of Ocean Motion.*
Coleman, Evelyn. *Freedom Train.*
Ferris, Jeri. *Arctic Explorer: The Story of Matthew Henson*
Frank, Anne. *The Diary of a Young Girl.*
Goodall, Jane. *My Life with the Chimpanzees.*
Hobbs, Will. *Jackie's Wild Seattle.*
Levine, Kristin. *The Lions of Little Rock.*
Lin, Grace. *Where the Mountain Meets the Moon.*
Montgomery, Sy. *Kakapo Rescue: Saving the World's Strangest Parrot.*
Montgomery, Sy and Temple Grandin. Temple Grandin: *How the Girl Who Loved Cows Embraced Autism and Changed the World.*

Montgomery, Sy. <u>Saving the Ghost of the Mountain</u>.

Mortenson, Greg. <u>Three Cups of Tea: One Man's Journey to Change the World One Child at a Time</u>.

Mowat, Farley. <u>Never Cry Wolf</u>.

Murphy, Jim. <u>An American Plague: The True And Terrifying Story of the Yellow Fever Epidemic of 1793</u>.

Nevola, Claire A. <u>Life in the Ocean: The Story of Oceanographer Sylvia Earle</u>.

Ottaviani, Jim. <u>Primates: The Fearless Science of Jane Goodall, Dian Fossey, and Birute Galdikas</u>.

Stone, Tanya Lee. <u>Almost Astronauts: 13 Women Who Dared to Dream</u>.

Swinburne, Stephen R. <u>Once A Wolf: How Wildlife Biologists Fought to Bring Back the Gray Wolf</u>.

Vanderpool, Clare. Moon Over Manifest.
Yousafzai, Malala and Christina Lamb. I Am Malala: The Girl Who Stood Up for Education and Was Shot by the Taliban.

References

Websites

file://localhost/(http/::www.cdc.gov:std:life-stages-populations:Adolescents-white-paper.pdf
"How to Talk to Your Middle Schooler". Moorman, Chuck.
tweenparenting.about.com

http://bullyfree.com/free-resources/facts-about-bullying
http://en.wikipedia.org/wiki/Kik_Messenger

http://journals.uic.edu/ojs/index.php/fm/article/view/3850/3075
http://samhsa.gov/data/NSDUH/2012SummNatFindDetTables/NationalFindings/NSDUHresults2012.htm#fig2.8

http://www.Ask.fm
http://www.amazon.com/author/kathleenbenyo.
http://www.commonsensemedia.org
http://www.drugabuse.gov/publications/drugfacts/high-school-youth-trends
http://www.drugabuse.gov/publications/media-guide/commonly-abused-drugs
http://www.Education.com/magazine/article/sixth_grade_math
http://www.Education.com/magazine/art/when-teens-talk-back
http://www.Education.com/magazine/art/when-teens-talk-back. Medoff, Lisa.

http://www.Education.com/magazine/art/when-teenagers-steal. Medoff, Lisa.
http://www.Education/magazine/art/when-teenagers-lie. Medoff, Lisa.
http://www.Facebook.com
http://www.fox.com
http://www.huffingtonpost.com/news/yik-yak
http://www.kik.com
http://www.netlingo.com/acronyms.php
http://www.psychologytoday. Darling, Nancy.
http://www.snapchat.com
http://www.thegrommet.com
http://www.Twitter.com

http://www.vine.co
http://www.YouTube.com

https://www.dosomething.org/facts/11-facts-about-bullying
https://www.snapchat.com/static_files/parents.pdf.
https://support.google.com/youtube/answer/174084?hl=en

Books

Erlbach, Arlene. The Middle School Survival Guide.
Farrell, Juliana, and Beth Mayall and Megan Howard. Middle School: The Real Deal.
Fox, Annie. Real Friends vs. the Other Kind: Middle School Confidential.
Hattie, Grandma. Middle School Survival Book.
Icard, Michelle. Middle School Makeover.

Lamadre, Claudia. <u>Middle School Survival Guide for Girls</u>.

Marks, Melanie. <u>Middle School Crushes</u>.

Natterson, Dr. Cara. <u>The Care and Keeping of You 2</u>.

Schaefer, Valorie and Josee Masse. <u>The Care and Keeping of You</u>.

Tobias. Cynthia. <u>Middle School: The Inside Story</u>.

Thank You ...

    For selecting this book. Your review would be appreciated so much. Each one is very helpful!

Acknowledgements

I owe my thanks to all of the great school leaders who offered me chances to be a leader myself. To Herb Kelshaw, the first principal who gave me my first teaching job. When I became a principal, I tried to emulate his leadership qualities. I hope I did him proud. To Dr. Richard Miller, who gave me my first break as a school administrator and taught me how to do my job. To special teachers – and there are many – who enabled me to hone my abilities as a school leader and offered honest feedback. I thank parents Gina Hoppes, Lorri Gavitt, and Katrina Molnar – among others -- for sharing some of their experiences with me about the crises their own daughters experienced. I thank my sister for taking the time to be my editor and best (and worst) critic and I love her for it. To my brother, whose amazing writing skills have encouraged me to improve my own. To my husband who has always encouraged me and expected me to be successful, thank you. Whether or not I reach that goal, it is heartwarming to know how much he believes in me.